THIRD IN A SERIES ON TEXAS BAPTIST LEADERS

The Bagbys *of* Brazil

The Life and Work of William Buck and Anne Luther Bagby

BY

DANIEL B. LANCASTER

EAKIN PRESS ★ Austin, Texas

Published in the United States of America
By Eakin Press
A Division of Sunbelt Media, Inc.
P.O. Box 90159 ★ Austin, Texas 78709
Email: eakinpub@sig.net
Website: www.eakinpress.com

2 3 4 5 6 7 8 9

ISBN 1-57168-251-1

Library of Congress Cataloging-in-Publication Data

Lancaster, Daniel B.
   The Bagbys of Brazil : the life and work of William Buck and Anne
Luther Bagby / by Daniel B. Lancaster.—1st ed.
      p.   cm.
   "Third in a series on Texas Baptist leaders."
   Includes bibliographical references and index.
   ISBN 1-57168-251-1
      1. Bagby, William Buck, b. 1885. 2. Bagby, Anne Ellen Luther, b. 1859
   3. Missionaries—Brazil—Biography. 4. Missionaries—Texas—Biography.
   5. Baptists—Brazil—Biography. 6. Baptists—Texas—Biography. I Title
BV2853.B7B335   1999
266'.61'0922--dc21   98-28967
                                                               CIP

To Holli,
Jeffrey, Zachary, Charis, and Zane:

God's promise to me.

Contents

Foreword

The saga of William Buck and Anne Luther Bagby is worth recounting. To "recount" means to tell again in a fresh, new form. That is what Dan Lancaster has done in this book. An earlier generation of Baptists was familiar with the story through the delightfully inspiring little book, *The Bagbys of Brazil*, by the late Helen Bagby Harrison—but a new generation of Baptists has arisen "that knows not the Bagbys!" This book is for them.

The story of the Bagbys is of special significance to several sectors of the evangelical community, especially Texas Baptists. Buck and Anne were scions of families which colonized Texas and generated the Baptist denomination. The Bagby story is also intertwined with the beginnings of Baylor University and Southwestern Baptist Seminary. Even more important, the Bagbys were pioneers in the fledgling foreign missions movement which gradually broke Texas Baptists out of their native provincialism. These characteristics insure this book a prominent place in this series on Texas Baptist leaders.

Dr. Lancaster chronicles the story simply and proudly, majoring on the personal and biographical. From letters, diaries, and memorabilia, deposited by the family in the libraries of Baylor University and Southwestern Seminary, Lancaster marshals the facts in a fluid, somewhat folksy style. Personal interviews with scattered relatives complement the academic research. The product is a work which avoids pedantry, without becoming a panegyric. Something of the heroic is present, but it plods along on feet of clay!

Like Texas, the Bagby story is big. They were pioneers in simple beginnings that resulted in large movements. Their persistence and perseverance contributed to the founding of some great Baptist institutions. They were ordinary people whose dedication to God's will led them to participate in some extra-ordinary events. Texas Baptist history bears the mark of the Bagbys.

First and foremost were their vision and diligence which resulted in the remarkable attainments of the Baptist witness in Brazil, which just happens to be the largest country in South America! Recruited by A. T. Hawthorne, a converted Confederate general who became the agent of the Foreign Mission Board in Texas, and sponsored by Texas Baptists under the leadership of B. H. Carroll, they responded to the call of a small colony of Confederate Baptists in Brazil. With a paucity of preparation and very limited resources, they, and their little band of national and missionary colleagues, laid the foundation for Southern Baptists' largest and most productive mission field.

Before leaving the mission field, Anne and Buck were involved in the founding and development of Texas Baptists' largest and most influential university. John Hill Luther, Anne's father, became president of Baylor College at Independence, Texas, in 1878, where Anne assisted him in the administration of the young school. William Buck was converted under the preaching of Rufus Burleson, who was the founder and first president of Waco University, which later merged with Baylor. Form these early contacts, the Bagby family bonded with Baylor. Several generations of Bagbys have attended and served "old Baylor." Bagby Street in Waco transverses the campus as a testimony to this relationship.

Southwestern Baptist Theological Seminary, the world's largest seminary, received the Bagby influence during its early days. B. H. Carroll, Southwestern's founder, was a close friend of the Bagbys. Buck was Carroll's first pupil in the Department of Theology at Waco University, which developed later into Southwestern Seminary. Bagby used to say, "Yes, Dr. Carroll and I founded the seminary. He was the faculty and I was the student body." Later, Carroll went on the road to raise funds from Texas Baptists to assure the Bagbys appointment. His daughter served a term as a missionary in Brazil.

The Bagbys missionary legacy transcended the United States of America and Brazil. Anne and Buck's daughter, Ermine, became the wife of the Southern Baptist pioneer missionary to Argentina, S. M. Sowell. Buck Bagby also was instrumental in bringing Chilean evangelicals, converted by W. D. T. McDonald, into the Baptist fold. The family's legacy is deposited in many South American countries. The wideness of their influence is impressive.

Dan Lancaster combines meticulous research with an appropriate writing style to relate the Bagby saga. Lancaster's style, like Lancaster himself, is low-key, but he does not overlook the human interest details which abound in the story. Dan Lancaster is a recent Ph.D. graduate of Southwestern Baptist Seminary. This is his first published work, crafted in the midst of a local church ministry. We hope it will not be his last.

JUSTICE C. ANDERSON
George W. Bottoms Professor of Missions
Director Emeritus, World Missions Center
Southwestern Baptist Theological Seminary
Fort Worth, Texas

Acknowledgments

The life and ministry of William Buck and Anne Luther Bagby fascinated me early in my doctoral work. The archives at Southwestern Baptist Theological Seminary included a collection of almost 1,600 folders of their correspondence, which documented their struggles and their triumphs. Sometimes laughing and other times crying, I gained a great deal of admiration for the Bagbys reading their epistles. I decided to present a fresh look at their influence and ministry—an objective historical approach in contrast to the tribute written by their youngest daughter, Helen Bagby Harrison. It was my privilege to be the first person to use the collection at Southwestern Baptist Theological Seminary extensively in my research. I also received a scholarship from the Southern Baptist Historical Society to study correspondence between the Bagbys and the Foreign Mission Board, housed in the Southern Baptist Archives, Nashville, Tennessee. In all, I examined more than 3,000 source documents for this work.

Several people aided in my research and deserve a word of appreciation: Dr. Alan J. Lefever, archivist, A. Webb Roberts Library, Southwestern Baptist Theological Seminary; Howard Gallimore, archivist, Southern Baptist Library and Archives; Edie Jeter, archivist, Foreign Mission Board, Southern Baptist Convention; Ellen Brown, archivist, The Texas Collection, Baylor University; Audrey Jiles, reference librarian, Townsend Memorial Library, Mary Hardin-Baylor University; and Dr. Karen Bullock, who categorized the Bagby-Luther Family Papers at Southwestern Seminary as an archival assistant, and recommended the study to the author.

Dr. H. Leon McBeth not only supervised the early part of my doctoral work, but also instilled a love for church history in me that has never abated. Thank you. Many thanks also go to Dr. Justice Anderson who agreed to supervise the project when Dr. McBeth took a sabbatic leave. A former Southern Baptist missionary to Argentina, it is both fitting and an honor that he wrote the foreword.

All of us need dear friends who make life happier and more fulfilling. I would like to thank the members of Community Bible Church, Hamilton, Texas; New Covenant Baptist Church, Temple, Texas; and Highland Fellowship, Lewisville, Texas; for their love and support during my doctoral work and the completion of this book.

But most of all, I would like to thank my wife and children for their love, faith, and confidence. Their patience and support while I pounded away at the keyboard encouraged me to finish the project. Holli, Jeffrey, Zachary, Charis, and Zane are one of the greatest sources of blessing I know.

Introduction

William Buck and Anne Luther Bagby served as Southern Baptist missionaries to Brazil from March 3, 1881, until August 5, 1939, a tenure surpassed only by one other missionary in the history of the Foreign Mission Board. The Bagbys organized the first Brazilian Baptist church with five members, but the work blossomed to 650 churches and 50,000 members by the time Will died in 1939. No other mission field reaped such a harvest for Southern Baptists, yet the Bagby story has only partially been told. Even less documented is the strong connection between Texas and Brazil.

It is surprising that little work has been done on the Bagbys considering the amount of primary source material that has survived. The Southern Baptist Archives and library in Nashville, Tennessee, house more than eight hundred letters between the Bagbys and the Foreign Mission Board. *The Bagby-Luther Family Papers* found at the Archives of the A. Webb Roberts Library at Southwestern Baptist Theological Seminary contain 1,576 folders and include personal mementos, mission tracts, correspondence between family members, and early publications by William Buck and Anne Luther Bagby. The Texas Collection at Baylor University holds the *Smith-Luther-Bagby Family Papers*—several hundred letters detailing the Bagbys ministry with their daughter and son-in-law in Porto Alegre, Rio Grande do Sul. Minutes of the committee on South American Missions, preserved in the Archives of the Southern Baptist Foreign Mission Board, also shed light on some problems and successes the Bagbys experienced. Letters and articles by the Bagbys give a unique view of more than fifty years of the Southern Baptist missionary enterprise.

Will and Anne both grew up in families dedicated to the

mission cause. Will's sister, Ermine, consecrated her life as a teenager to the mission cause, and ultimately fulfilled her calling by writing Will encouraging letters from home. His mother dedicated him to the gospel ministry as a small child, and named him after William C. Buck, a famous Southern Baptist missionary. Anne bore the namesake of another famous missionary, Ann Judson. Stories by her father of a lost opportunity to minister in Africa seem to have propelled Anne toward more than half a century of mission work. He had not gone, but she did.

The Bagbys first ministered to a colony of ex-confederates in Santa Barbara, Brazil. Problems with alcoholism, drug abuse, and other social vices among the colonists blocked their missionary attempts. Even when the board sent Z. C. and Kate Taylor as reinforcements, the gospel fell on rocky soil. The couples decided to move their work away from the Americans, and pursue evangelizing the Brazilians. Their motto was "don't despise the day of small things."

The Bagbys and Taylors moved the mission to Salvador, Bahia, and began to experiment with different methods to reach the masses. They soon found that Brazilians professed conversion one person at a time—mass evangelism did not work. Accounts of persecution by Catholic priests bolstered the Baptist cause, however, and sold newspapers in the United States as well. Money and people began to trickle from Texas to Brazil, but a rift between the Bagbys and Taylors almost extinguished the effort.

The rift began to heal when the Bagbys moved from Salvador to Rio de Janeiro, but numeric results were dour until the revolution of 1889. Then, with the rise of a pro-democracy sentiment, Baptist work in Brazil ignited. Churches and associations sprang up, and new territories were secured. In the midst of such optimism, however, disease decimated the missionary ranks. The cold bodies of young men and women filled foreign graves and challenged the resolve of the Bagbys.

After almost twenty years in Rio de Janeiro, the Bagbys moved to Sao Paulo City, Sao Paulo, in 1901. It was in Sao Paulo that the Bagbys began to see a fruitful harvest from years of steady toil. Anne organized a school for girls, which became the flagship for Southern Baptists in Brazil. Will influenced the board to build a college and seminary in Rio de Janeiro, and led in the organization of the first national Brazilian convention. The Bagbys ardent spirit anchored the uneasy wedding between evangelistic passion and educational purposes.

In the midst of incredible success, the Bagbys engaged in conflict over a school situation in their twilight years of ministry. When Harley and Alice Bagby Smith encountered trouble with missionary A. L. Dunstan, Will and Anne moved to Porto Allegre, Rio Grande do Sul, to defend their daughter and son-in-law. Their presence in the field, however, created problems that spread to the entire South Brazil mission. Ironically, the same hard-fisted, win-at-any-cost attitude that allowed the Bagbys to lay a strong foundation in their early years of ministry, frustrated them at the end of their ministry.

Will and Anne Bagby became foreign missionaries at a time of extraordinary transformation in the southern part of the United States. The role of women began to change dramatically during the Bagbys' ministry, and Anne Luther Bagby became a lightning rod for missions among Baptist women in Texas. After the Foreign Mission Board appointed the Bagbys, Texas assumed a significant role in foreign missions, and the offering plates for foreign fields overflowed, even in times of drought. The Bagbys were the progenitors of what has become, in many ways, the most successful foreign mission enterprise of the Southern Baptist Convention. Following the example of Baptists on the American frontier, they organized churches, associations, schools, colleges, seminaries, and a convention in Brazil. Contemporaries credited the Bagbys as the decisive trailblazers of Southern Baptist mission work in Brazil. This is their story.

Chapter 1

Missionary Heritage

No one was surprised when Dr. John Luther preached on foreign missions that Sunday night. It was his custom. Most members of the church knew that the missionary call had been a theme of his life. As a young man, he had decided to go to Africa after an inspiring meeting with T. J. Bowen and applied to the Foreign Mission Board of the Southern Baptist Convention. Later, however, he wrote the board to withdraw his name from consideration. He felt like poor health and a lack of teaching ability were two insurmountable obstacles.

"God has blessed America and we must share that blessing with the world!" he proclaimed to the congregation. His own sense of inadequacy seemed to fuel the message on. "So few dedicate their lives to God on such a high sphere. Such consecration is only for God's choicest servants. If you go, remember we will always be here supporting you in prayer on our knees. You will not be forgotten!" The sermon crescendoed at the end in one final "Who will go?"

In his usual way, Dr. Luther offered an invitation to those needing salvation or desiring to commit themselves to mission service. The congregation began softly to sing an invitation hymn. That night only one came forward . . . Luther's twelve-year-old daughter Anne. "Child," he quietly stammered, "I didn't mean you!"

ANNE ELLEN LUTHER

Anne's father, John Hill Luther, aspired early in his life to be a missionary to Africa after a meeting with Southern Baptist missionary T. J. Bowen.[1] Luther applied to the Foreign Mission

1

Board, but his dream did not materialize because of poor health and dissatisfaction with his teaching ability. He wrote the board asking the corresponding secretary to remove his name as a candidate.

Relieved by his son's decision not to go to Africa, Luther's father encouraged him to convert the slaves in the southern United States instead. Following his father's advice, he took a preaching position at the Black Swamp Church in South Carolina. He preached ". . . three times a week to the slaves on plantations owned by Baptists, Methodists, and Infidels . . . and buried in baptism a large number of Negroes and sons and daughters of the plantation owners."[2] The church was composed of wealthy planters, and it also had a strong Methodist element which persecuted the young pastor for abolitionist articles he had written.

Luther boarded with Ben Jaudon during his pastorate at the Black Swamp Church and began to court Ben's sixteen-year-old daughter, Ann. Their marriage on August 3, 1854, was a magnificent affair, and "even the Negroes were remembered."[3] The young couple soon moved to Pendleton, North Carolina, and ministered to a church composed entirely of women. Luther later wrote, "The year I passed there was one of the happiest years of my life."[4]

Luther's missionary aspirations continued to haunt him, prompting him to accept a commission to go to the Kansas territory and start Baptist churches. He quickly discovered, however, that starting Baptist schools was easier than starting Baptist churches. The Luther family settled in Kansas City and established a school for girls. They constructed the school from part of his wife's inheritance, and the institute thrived.

After the death of their first child, the Luthers celebrated the birth of Anne Ellen Luther on March 20, 1859. They named Anne after her mother, who was named for Ann Hasseltine Judson, the wife of foreign missionary Adoniram Judson.[5] Being named after Judson had a significant impact on Anne's later desire to become a missionary.[6]

The economic collapse of the South during the Civil War led to the ruin of Luther's school in Kansas City. Because of John's sympathy with the slaves, the Luther family moved from

Kansas City, Kansas, to Miami, Missouri. Although promised protection in Miami, they left the city because John felt uncomfortable "when prominent citizens were shot down in cold blood" near their home.[7] They retreated to Quincy, Illinois, to live near relatives. At each location, the Luther family was forced to leave because of convictions concerning the Civil War. Luther supported the slaves in their efforts toward freedom and was consequently considered a "northerner" by some. But he also supported the south's call for economic equality and secession and thus was considered a "southerner" by others. It is not surprising, then, that little Anne often took wagon rides with soldiers from both sides of the war and cheered them with songs on the piano in the family parlor.

The Luther family moved to St. Louis, Missouri, when John accepted a position as editor of the *Central Baptist* and became the pastor of the Carondolet Baptist Church in 1870. It was at this church that Anne professed salvation at the age of eleven. She demanded to be baptized immediately, although she had recently suffered from pneumonia. Her parents agreed after some persuasion, and John Hill Luther baptized her in the Mississippi River as "the last of its icy sheet disappeared."[8] A steamer came by at the time of her baptism and almost drowned Anne in its wake, but her father rescued her quickly. Anne shivered uncontrollably in her father's arms but no illness resulted from the baptism.[9]

Anne's final call to foreign missions came six years later during her senior year at Lexington Baptist College in Missouri. After hearing a missionary from Africa speak in chapel, she initiated plans for mission work and began to correspond with missionaries in Burma.[10]

Luther was forced to sell the *Central Baptist* after it fell on difficulties due to the poor management of one of his business partners. Discouraged and depressed, Luther left the Carondolet Baptist Church. He found it impossible to live in the city where he had suffered the loss of a newspaper he had built from the ground up. He moved to Fe Fe and served as pastor of a Baptist church for two years. Several derogatory remarks toward his wife made by some women of the Fe Fe church crystallized his decision to move again.[11]

Luther then served for one year as pastor of Second Baptist Church at Galveston, and Anne helped him by playing the organ. After healing a rift in the church in Galveston, he accepted the presidency of Baylor Female College at Independence, Texas, in 1879.[12] According to Luther, Baylor Female College "for many years had been a prosperous institution, but it had run down [*sic*] and I was persuaded to enter upon what seemed to be a forlorn hope."[13]

The Luthers' first year at Independence was successful. Anne even helped organize a campus-wide skip day in the spring semester.[14] John served not only as president of the college, but also as Lecturer of Moral and Intelligence Philosophy and Ancient Languages.[15] By 1881 the college had 125 students, fifty of whom were boarders. The next year six women graduated.[16]

Anne taught English, literature, and mathematics at the college and served as head-assistant and matron of the boarding house. She wrote:

> I never before was kept so constantly employed: waking to ring the study bell, inspecting the rooms, teaching some of Pa's classes . . . presiding over the study hall at night, and fulfilling various other tasks.[17]

She stood five feet tall, weighed ninety-two pounds, wore her dresses long, and fashioned her brunette hair in tight rolls like a seamstress to look older. The students,

> . . . enjoyed the comradeship of this young teacher but gave her due respect. "She's great fun," one would say. "But strict in school," someone would add. "You'd never think she was going to be a missionary," was a frequent comment among the girls. "Not when she puts her arms in boots and sings 'Little Brown Jug, Don't I love Thee.'" "She cries at night," another would aver, "because she's got to be a missionary and she doesn't want to leave her mother and father." "Who makes her go then?" persists the first. "God," answers the other with the finality of youth.[18]

Her youthful enthusiasm made her a favorite of all the students. Some of Anne's methods drew sharp criticism from members of the community, however. She enjoyed orchestrating dramatic skits and musical concerts with her pupils, but her critics accused her of doing the concerts solely to display her beautiful singing voice. Another frequent accusation was that she had usurped the role of president of the college and commanded everyone, including her father. In an era of emerging rights for women, Anne's strong personality met with stiff resistance.[19]

Her desire to hold Sunday School for former slaves in the community opened fresh moral wounds and caused the greatest criticism. Anne continued in her efforts, however, because she believed it was necessary training for the foreign mission field. She wrote, ". . . a young lady and myself and three of the university students have commenced teaching in the Colored Sunday School, Sabbath afternoons. We enjoy it ever so much. It seems to me that I am nearer my future home when in their poor meeting house."[20] Because of her desire to become a foreign missionary, Anne continued to correspond regularly with as many as thirty-two individuals expressing an interest in missions, and she participated in denominational activities as well.[21]

WILLIAM BUCK BAGBY

William Buck Bagby's parents, James Henry and Mary Franklin Bagby, began their married life together in Louisville, Kentucky, in 1843.[22] Mary was the daughter of John S. Willson, pastor of the First Baptist Church of Louisville, Kentucky. Willson died of a heart attack while preaching a Sunday night service. Shortly afterward, Mary and her two sisters decided to move their families to Texas. They traveled by river boat to New Orleans, then by steamer along the Gulf of Mexico to Galveston, and finally by oxcart to Coryell County in central Texas. They settled near Hog Creek in January 1852 and called their new family farm "Prairie Home." They built three crude houses close together for protection from Indian raids.[23]

Texas was still a rugged, untamed land with occasional attacks from the Comanche Indians, but eventually the settlers initiated trade, and peace prevailed with the neighboring Indians. William Bagby later remembered the area as ". . . a romantic region of prairies and woodlands, of hills and valleys, of cedars, live oaks, and elms. The prairies in the spring and summer were gay with flowers, and the woodlands, ravines, and valleys held treasures of berries of many kinds, wild haws, mustang grapes, and wild plums."[24]

Religious piety characterized the Bagby home, and it soon became a frequent stopping place for preachers and evangelists.[25] Mary Bagby taught her neighbors the Bible, and when William Buck Bagby was born on November 5, 1855, "it was her expressed desire and prayer that her son should preach."[26] She named him after a famous Southern Baptist missionary and relative, William C. Buck, who had succeeded her father as pastor of First Baptist Church in Louisville, Kentucky. William Bagby was the last of five children born into the Bagby home and was preceded by Henry Dudley, Luther William, Ermine, and James Franklin Bagby. His childhood nickname was "Willie."

William Bagby's evangelistic career began early. As a three-year-old, he held church services, preaching to the dining room chairs. He would become angry when family members moved the chairs because he did not want people "disturbing his church." He also practiced homiletics on captive barnyard animals and became incensed if anyone opened the gate and allowed his parishioners to escape. He frequently listened to his sister Ermine speak of her desire to be a foreign missionary and heard many Southern Baptist home missionaries sharing their spiritual victories on the Texas frontier.[27]

The Bagbys left Coryell County in 1862 and moved to the east side of Waco, Texas, to establish a general merchandise store. When the railroad came, it connected Waco with other cities in Texas, and the store owned by the Bagbys prospered as a result. In fact, city leaders named two streets in Waco after the Bagbys, who became social pillars in the community.[28]

The Bagbys found sorrow and success mingled in Waco, however. Henry, William's oldest brother, was killed in combat during the Civil War, and Luther returned a semi-invalid. Although Luther "was very fond of the society of women, he felt that he should afflict no women with an unsound husband, so he died a bachelor."[29]

William Bagby's experiences in Waco foretold grander adventures in the future. He attended a public school taught by his cousin, Mary Halbert Buck, and geography quickly became his favorite subject. Four of the places in the world he most wanted to see were: the Andes, the Amazon River, the Pampas of Argentina, and Rio de Janeiro, Brazil.[30] The Bagby family attended First Baptist Church, Waco, and William's favorite Sunday School teacher as a child was Colonel Speight. During a revival meeting in 1868 at the church, he professed conversion and R. C. Burleson baptized him.

In 1873 William entered Waco University and was the only student of theology for a short time. He often claimed that he and Dr. B. H. Carroll were the first Southwestern Baptist Theological Seminary—with Dr. Carroll the faculty and he the student body.[31]

While studying at Waco University William Bagby developed a friendship with Z. C. Taylor, a young man who had come to Waco to study medicine. They practiced their speaking skills as members of the Philomathesian Society and shared the same dream of preaching the gospel.[32] Both listened to gifted preachers like R. C. Burleson, William C. Buck, and B. H. Carroll. Taylor planned to minister on the foreign field while William wanted a church position in America where his literary skills would be more appreciated in English. He wanted "to combine spirituality with eloquence in the pulpit."[33] William sharpened his academic skills by editing *The Texas Literary Guardian* his last year at Waco University.

William graduated from Waco University in 1875, hoping to secure a pastorate or teaching position. Several church leaders in Waco made a motion to license him to preach, but they deferred the matter to a later time.[34] Due to a shortage of teaching positions, he moved to Coryell County and farmed with his Uncle Bland for a year. Soon he became a superintendent of the Sunday School at Eagle Springs, and the Onion Creek Church finally licensed him to preach on May 5, 1877.[35]

Obtaining a dependable teaching job proved difficult for William. Education in Texas during this period was as rugged as the frontier itself: "Communities did not build adequate schoolhouses, teachers were not qualified, and the rural school term was approximately four months long."[36] No consistent system of public education existed, so many communities hired an instructor to teach a "free" school for several months with the hope that the community would see the school's benefit and support it afterward. The usual outcome, however, was that no school was formed, and the teacher would move on to try again in another city. William taught school at Wallace's Prairie and Whitehall, but he was forced to move on when the communities were not forthcoming with financial support.

William's third attempt at a teaching position in Texas was successful. Moving to Courtney, he boarded with a wealthy member of the church who had influence in the community. With his characteristic wit, William reported to his mother that "he probably would not starve" as a result.[37] He was full of optimism, saying, "My boarding house is just a good 15 minute walk from the school house. . . . The free school will last only three months but I think the people will support a good private school after the free term is over."[38]

His hopes for a sustained private school came to pass. Along with teaching, he served as pastor at First Baptist Church, Courtney, and assisted in organizing their first Sunday School.[39] He also established a Literary Society in the community.[40]

At this point, William began to consider furthering his theological education at Southern Baptist Seminary in Louisville, Kentucky. His interest in Sunday School work, however, drew him to the first Sunday School convention in Texas on a bright July morning in 1878.

COURTSHIP

Sunday School work in Texas was in its infancy, and Baptists organized a statewide convention at Calvert to educate and train new workers in July 1878. Churches sent messengers to the convention, and First Baptist Church, Courtney, nominated William Buck Bagby to go. Anne Luther also attended, representing Second Baptist Church, Galveston. Anne described their first impressions of each other:

> At the first meeting I saw in the front of the church a young man whose eyes always met mine, and after the close of the

session had the pleasure of an introduction to him. The convention closed all too soon, and as we prepared for our home-going, I remarked that my only regret was that I had not become acquainted with a certain young minister. What was our surprise when a note was handed to me at the next moment requesting an immediate interview . . . I must have done all the talking, for I spoke of my desire, even purpose, of becoming a foreign missionary. I told him I tried to write poetry, and gave him a copy of the *Central Baptist* which had printed one of my rhymes . . . Later I met him at the railroad station. I was bound for the south, he for the north, but he missed his train . . . Shortly after reaching home, I received a letter addressed in an unfamiliar hand. I eagerly opened it, to find that it was from the young preacher, asking that I correspond with him and giving in reference to his character the names of a number of prominent ministers. It sent me to my knees and then to my father, who gravely said, "If you consent to this request you will receive a proposal in less than three months." Well . . . I wrote.[41]

Thus began a relationship that influenced thousands of people in both Texas and Brazil.

It was shortly after the convention that the Luther family moved to Independence, and William and Anne began to develop their relationship through correspondence. Courtney was thirty-six miles away from Independence, a long journey by horseback, but Will began to visit Anne on the weekends, once a month. After their initial meeting Anne wrote, "I was not aware that I talked otherwise than with my tongue but one thing I do know you talked with your eyes and that the language, though foreign to me, was most eloquent."[42] She added, "I must be a foreign missionary! It is my daily prayer that this, which has been the brightest, saddest light in my pathway, may not be extinguished."[43] A month later she shared, "You are the only one who has ever rang the cheery chimes of love in my heart's dome."[44] Several suitors had tried, however, including her vocal instructor and Z. C. Taylor.[45]

Taylor had quit his studies at Waco University for financial reasons and sold books in the Waco area to raise money for his tuition. He revived his studies after hearing a missionary from China speak during chapel at Waco University, and came to Baylor College for Men at Independence in 1878. He planned to commence missionary work in Brazil and wrote H. A. Tupper, corresponding secretary of the Southern Baptist Foreign Mission Board, concerning his ideas. Z. C. and Anne spent many afternoons together talking about the mission field, and he purchased a copy of *Brazil and the Brazilians*, by Kier and Fletcher, for her to read.[46] His advances became a source of embarrassment for Anne, however, and she severed the relationship abruptly. The end of the relationship caused Taylor to become severely ill and a "perfect hermit" for several months.[47]

Anne's aspirations for the mission field had made her a statewide heroine for the mission cause. When H. A. Tupper visited Z. C. Taylor in March of 1879, he requested an interview with Anne, too. She was hesitant to speak to him but honored Tupper's request because of his social standing. Tupper affirmed her missionary call and talked to her about the work in Burma.[48] In a fitting tribute to his daughter, John Hill Luther commissioned an artist from Galveston to paint a full-size portrait of Anne. In the background were the natives of Burma and a church shining out of the darkness. Anne's father proudly displayed the portrait at Baylor College for Women.[49]

Anne soon discovered a dark side to the missionary call, however. Women who volunteered for missionary service acquired a mythical quality among their peers, a fact that made Anne uncomfortable. She received several requests to speak as a future missionary and wrote to Will after one such occasion saying, "I am appointed to read an essay at the Chappell Hill Convention. Why won't people let me alone!"[50] After the convention she confessed, "Mr. Kendrick urges me write and publish often. He says I have no right to keep so quiet . . . Oh, but I am so deficient. You all don't know me! Indeed, you don't."[51] She feared scrutinizing eyes that would scour her mission articles looking for mistakes, sneering at her attempts.

Anne struggled with the missionary persona and her relationship with Will. She reprimanded him for sending her postcards because anyone could read the outside of the card and gossip. She seethed with anger when he kissed her hand, snarling, "it would insult me if Pa should offer to kiss my hand and how much more should it offend me for a gentleman to do so . . . my sensitive disposition and my peculiar position forbids that I should countenance the act."[52] Anne was embarrassed to be seen with Will in public, especially at conventions. She believed somehow it might tarnish her reputation and the public's perception of her mission.

The main obstacle that Will and Anne faced in their relationship was her call to foreign missions and his call to pastor in America. Early in their relationship, Will continued his plan to attend Southern Seminary in Louisville, Kentucky. Anne decided she would follow him there, asserting that having an education on the foreign field was just as important for a woman as a man.[53] But as their relationship grew, both began to wrestle more with Anne's missionary call. They were engaged to be married during Christmas 1879, although they had not settled the issue. Anne wrote Will's mother:

> I cannot remember the time, of course, that I did not have a preference for some youth, but I can honestly say that I never loved in earnest until I met your son; and he was the first who told me of his love. Really I did not mean to love him. I had always feared, up to the time of my meeting him, that I might love someone. I really did try not to love him, but I do love him. I believe that God means for me to love him.
>
> Should our paths lie in different directions, my affection, I am convinced, would never be withdrawn from the object to which it now clings. The fate of my heart is sealed, and must remain so, since God permits me to retain my present conscientious sentiments. . . .[54]

The issue began to resolve itself in the following months, however, as Will began to feel a burden for the heathens in Burma. Anne wrote Will, "I am willing to go anywhere except to Africa."[55]

This development led the young couple to formulate a different plan. Will readjusted his ambition to attend Southern Seminary and decided instead to go to Newton Seminary in Philadelphia, believing that appointment by the American Baptists was a greater possibility. Anne prepared to go to medical school in Boston with financial backing from the American Baptist Foreign Mission Board.[56] Fannie Breedlove's mother also offered to pay her way.[57] Anne had already written the American Baptist Foreign Mission Board requesting an application for foreign missionary.[58]

The couple's plan to pursue appointment with the American Baptists better suited Anne's parents. They were concerned that Will and Anne probably could not wait for two more years before getting married.[59] Quickly moving toward her lifetime intent, Anne wrote, "I do long to be lost in Christ! Oh, how I do yearn for his continual presence! Must I wait until I have reached heathen lands ere I know the bliss of walking on earth in the atmosphere of Heaven?"[60]

Chapter 2

The Fourth Attempt

The aging missionary opened his fraying Bible and began to speak to the assembled crowd. He had given the simple message a hundred times. "Hopefully there will be a good offering today," he thought to himself. Money was scarce now. The Civil War had ended eight years before, but the pockets of most in the South were still empty.

He talked about evangelistic work among the heathen Yoruba tribes. Tears streamed down his face as he reflected on how much it had cost him —his health, his family, his reputation. He pleaded with the people to give of themselves like he had done. If not with their lives, at least with their money. "It is our destiny!" he said, his voice beginning to rise. "America is a light on a hill. We are called to reach the heathen with the gospel of Christ!"

He finished the sermon and staggered back to his seat beside the pastor. It looked like he carried the weight of the world on his shoulders. No one could deny he had paid an awful price. The young children looked at him with a mixture of admiration and pity.

The congregation sung a hymn while the offering plate was passed. It took longer than usual . . . a good sign he decided. He could tell the whole town had anticipated this meeting for weeks. All the churches of Courtney had gathered at First Baptist Church to hear him. The atmosphere was festive and reverent. He liked it that way.[1]

At the end of the service, people pressed into him asking questions, making comments, shaking hands with T. J. Bowen, former Southern Baptist missionary to Africa and Brazil.

Bowen was not disappointed that afternoon when the pastor gave him the missionary offering. It was larger than usual. "People in Texas give better than any other state in the South," he concluded. At least now

13

he would have money to continue his speaking tour. And there was enough for whiskey too.

"So this is what my life has come to," he pondered as he rode out of Courtney. "Speaking at old friend's churches, taking collections, spending it on travel and whiskey. They only invited me because they feel sorry for me." Then the old thoughts that had almost sent him to the asylum began to resurface and he hastily took out his old friend from the saddle bag and they kissed again.

A few years later, T. J. Bowen died in a sanitarium—a lonely and broken man.

THE BOWEN AFFAIR

Twenty years before the arrival of the Bagbys, Southern Baptist missionary T. J. Bowen had ventured to Brazil. He had served initially as a Southern Baptist missionary to Africa, but was forced to return to the United States because of health problems.[2] After several years of repeated attempts to return to Africa, Bowen developed a plan to start a mission in Brazil. His main reason for going was "to educate 'colored' preachers to be sent to Africa."[3] Many slaves in Brazil were from Yoruba, the region in Africa that Bowen had attempted to evangelize. On October 11, 1859, Bowen offered himself as a missionary to Brazil with plans to form two congregations in Rio de Janeiro, Brazil: one that spoke English, and the other that spoke Yoruba. The board consented, and Bowen, along with his wife Lurana, set sail for Brazil.

The Bowens encountered trouble shortly after their arrival in Rio de Janeiro. Government officials became alarmed when Bowen began to organize the Yoruba church. They believed he was organizing a slave revolt, and intense persecution followed. Bowen complained they were, ". . . shunned as heretics, condemned to silence by penal laws, hated by a people who are merciless in speaking evil of each other, without society or associates, and a gloomy prospect before us, we both feel that we have never been so unhappy."[4]

Bowen also critiqued the field, saying, ". . . to establish the gospel in a heathen country is like clearing a heavy forest and raising a crop, but to establish it in a Catholic country is like entering the same forest full of fierce savages who must be subdued before you clear the land."[5] Bowen speculated that the gospel might be most effectively introduced to the Brazilians through informal conversations and the distribution of tracts and books.[6]

Already suffering from poor health, the persecution took its toll and on February 6, 1860, Lurana wrote the board that the Bowens were leaving Brazil. Her husband was failing in mind and body, and she had arranged to leave without his knowledge or consent.[7] On February 7, 1860, the Bowens sailed from Rio for Baltimore, and the first foreign mission attempt by Southern Baptists in Brazil came to a hasty conclusion. Bowen spent his remaining years separated from his wife, wandering across the United States, supported by the benevolent offerings of churches in which he spoke.

CONFEDERATE EXILES

The great chasm T. J. Bowen encountered between American Protestant culture and Brazilian society was fueled by ignorance. In fact, Brazilians in the nineteenth century were far more interested in news from Europe than from the United States. Only significant American events, like the assassination of a president, might show up in their newspapers, and then perhaps three or four days after the incident. One American reported from Brazil that, "a leading journal publishes a tolerably fair letter from a New York correspondent once about every two months: but the same journal prints seventy-five letters from Europe to every one that it prints from the United States."[8]

The result of such meager communication between Brazil and the United States was a great deal of blurred information between the two nations. One lucid fact did emerge during the Civil War of the United States: Brazil backed the southern states and their cause. This is a little surprising in light of the fact that the southern states had considered forming new "slave" states in Brazil to strengthen their "slavocrat bloc" in the United States Congress.[9] Indeed, "in this era, the fingers of manifest destiny pointed southward as frequently as westward."[10] Scanty communication allowed both nations to believe the other had its best interests in mind.

With the loss of the Civil War came harsh new realities in the southern United States. Rumors of murderous gangs raping and pillaging former slave owners, carpet baggers, and economic disaster were only some mementos of a war fought between friends and brothers. The situation was dire: "Here and there despondency was so great that individuals resorted to the extremity of taking their own lives, while in every community discouragement made many eager to desert the land of their birth."[11]

Within four months of the surrender at Appomattox, a New York paper reported that 50,000 southerners were ready to emigrate to Brazil. "The leading journals of the Brazilian empire ventured to predict that 100,000 families of prominent, virtuous, and intelligent people, chiefly from the states recently in rebellion, would seek homes in their country."[12] Newspapers of the period declared there to be as great an interest in moving to Brazil and other South American countries, as there was in pushing to the far western United States.[13]

The Brazilian government assigned agents to New York and New Orleans to solicit those dissatisfied enough to venture to a new country.[14] These agents advertised heavily in the newspapers and spoke often before interested groups. Their offers were not always accurate, but they were always hard to resist. The agents reported enthusiastically the unsurpassed fertility of Brazil and her beautiful landscape. They also arranged for prospecting agents to visit Brazil with the hopes of inducing testimonies that would spur others to move.[15]

Several groups representing people from almost every social and economic class in the United States organized to emigrate to Brazil: "There were generals, colonels, doctors, lawyers, merchants, planters, ministers, teachers, barroom loafers, bounty jumpers, and vagabonds."[16] Advertisements soliciting colonists warned that no persons would be considered unless "they would qualify morally and politically . . . that is be southerners and hold pro-slavery sentiments."[17] Major colonies were started in four regions: Santarem, Para, Espiritu Santo, and Sao Paulo. The only colony that proved to be permanent was the one in the interior of Sao Paulo at Santa Barbara. Five hundred American families lived there at its peak.[18]

The Santa Barbara colonists cultivated beans, corn, cotton, sugar cane, and became successful cattle breeders. Their best crop, however, was watermelon. A colonist brought seeds from the United States, and the Brazilians preferred the newer variety to their own.[19] Those willing to endure strenuous labor found Brazil accurately portrayed by the newspaper pitch men and immigration agents. The majority of the optimistic Americans, however, cursed the advertisements and returned home.

Slavery never became a significant reality among the American colonists, although the Brazilian government allowed them to own slaves. The immigration laws of Brazil prohibited "the introduction of Negroes from the United States," and so the colonists were wholly dependent upon the purchase of Brazilian slaves. They soon discovered "that the nature and the laws and social customs of Brazil had made of the Brazilian Negro a very different creature."[20] Most of the slaves would simply flee back to the city from which they were bought after a few days of work.

Several colonists organized a Baptist church on September 10, 1871, under the leadership of Reverend Richard Ratcliff. Twenty-three adults from various Baptist churches in the southern United States united to form "the First North American Baptist Missionary Church of Brazil."[21] Having established their settlement and experienced some economic success, Baptist colonists in Santa Barbara began to discuss the possibility of receiving missionaries from the United States to serve their church and convert the native population.[22]

The colonists appointed three men as officers to communicate with the Southern Baptist Board of Foreign Missions at Richmond, Virginia, regarding sending missionaries to Brazil.[23] They wrote the board, asserting that, "Five or six years experience and intercourse with citizens of this country enables us to state that now is a propitious time to set forth the religion taught in God's word to this people."[24] The colonists believed the Brazilians to be open to Protestantism, saying, "Generally, they do not like their religion, saying 'it begins and ends with money for the priesthood.'"[25] At that point, the committee knew of only three Baptist preachers in all of Brazil and petitioned for reinforcements.[26]

Their pleas for help fell on warm hearts but cold pocketbooks. Unfortunately, the Civil War had crippled the finances of the Foreign Mission Board, and the possibility of beginning a new work could only be considered unrealistic thinking. Bowen's fiasco presented yet another reason to delay support. The board answered the supplication of the committee suggesting that financial support of a missionary was impossible but they would offer prayers to God for them. The board did consent, however, to the appointment of a missionary if his salary be supported by the colony.[27] Richard Ratcliff served as a Southern Baptist missionary to Brazil for the next five years until the death of his wife forced his return to the United States to find someone to care for his children.[28] The second attempt by a Southern Baptist missionary had failed.

Ratcliff wrote the board after his arrival in Mexia, Texas, recommending a new missionary be appointed to Brazil. He suggested that E. H. Quillen be selected, saying, "Their present pastor authorized me to say to the Board, that he would accept an appointment to the Brazilians . . . and make quarterly reports to the Board, without charging one cent. I ask the Board to open correspondence with him at once."[29] The board accepted this suggestion and appointed Quillen as a self-supporting missionary in 1879. E. H. Quillen had come with the original settlers of Santa Barbara as a pastor from Hillsboro, Texas.[30]

The third attempt by Southern Baptists to establish a foreign mission in Brazil looked bright and promising. However, the personal problems of the new pastor crushed the opportunity. Quillen suffered from a club foot and became addicted to the sedatives prescribed to stop the pain. His drug addiction ultimately led to alcoholism. He was frequently irrational, rarely preached, and developed marginal ideas concerning mission work. The church split into two factions under his leadership, and the third attempt to establish a Baptist mission in Brazil began to dissipate in discouragement and hopelessness among the colonists at Santa Barbara.[31] However, out of the colony of Santa Barbara there arose a man whose passion would propel many missionaries to Brazil.

GENERAL A. T. HAWTHORNE

Major Penn was a famous Southern Baptist evangelist in the two decades following the Civil War and was often called "the Dwight L. Moody of Texas."[32] He preached hard against sin and saw many converts. After attending one of his revival meetings during her time at Independence, Texas, Anne Luther decided Penn's methods would touch only the sordid sort from society.[33] It was at one of Penn's meetings in Marshall, Texas, in 1879, that an aging Confederate general came forward and professed conversion. He was struggling with alcoholism and the death of one of his children.[34] His name was A. T. Hawthorne.

A. T. Hawthorne had traveled to Brazil after the Civil War and helped establish the colony at Santa Barbara. It was on a return trip to Texas to canvass more colonists that he was converted. Now a transformed man, Brazil weighed heavily on his heart as a compelling mission field, and he set about to educate and motivate Southern Baptists concerning the potential spiritual gold mine. In 1880 he appeared before the Southern Baptist Convention meeting in Lexington, Kentucky, and made an appeal to send missionaries to Brazil. The results were positive: "So well impressed was the Convention with the personality, the intelligent insight and spiritual fervor of Hawthorne, that they appointed him an agent of the Foreign Mission Board in Texas."[35]

Soon after he returned from the Southern Baptist Convention, Hawthorne visited Baylor College for Women, seeking an appointment with the president's daughter. He wished to speak to her about Brazil. Before his death in 1899, Hawthorne would be responsible for sending fifteen missionaries from Texas to Brazil.[36] On a quiet night in June, Anne became his first convert.

Anne informed Hawthorne she was engaged and asked him to talk to William also. She then quickly wrote her fiancee, inquiring,

> What do you think? General A. T. Hawthorne wishes me to go immediately to Brazil as a missionary. He thinks I could there pursue the study of medicine, at the same time that I was acquiring the language. He pronounces the people pleasant—the government favorable to Christianity—the climate fine. . . . And you know how hard Mr. Taylor pled for that country.

> Pa is greatly in favor of my choosing it for my home and Ma
> and Aunt Addie approve of the same. So it seems to me that
> the finger of Providence points just in that direction. Now what
> of the time? . . . I feel that I would be better satisfied to enter
> immediately upon the work. I have always been afraid of delay.
> I do not wish to interfere with any of your plans. They tell me
> that I can go alone but that it would be far better to be mar-
> ried. . . . I have been thinking it would be far better for me to
> go while my memory is fresh in the minds of my pupils and
> friends if I must look to them for support. . . . I shall always
> look back upon my life in Texas as being the happiest part of
> my existence. The friends I have made here are, I believe, to
> be strong and lasting.[37]

Anne encouraged William to meet with Hawthorne and to re-
consider his plan to attend Newton Seminary, asserting, "if you
go to a Northern school the Southern people will never forget
it."[38] She, however, desired him to make his own decision: "I wish
you to find out just exactly what is best to do at the Convention
by consulting the General and Pa and your own feelings. Leave
me out of the question entirely."[39]

William met with Hawthorne and was impressed with his
passion for Brazil. They became quick friends. He wrote his sister Ermine a few weeks later saying, "I have entirely given up the
idea of going to the Orient for Brazil. . . . General Hawthorne
urges myself and Miss Anne to go out at once to that field and
discourages my contemplated course at Louisville."[40] William applied the next day to the Foreign Mission Board of the Southern
Baptist Convention for both Anne and himself.[41] After consulta-
tion with General Hawthorne, he asked the board to allow the
couple to fill the vacancy in the work in Santa Barbara.[42] William
wrote Anne, "I am ready to go to Brazil as soon as the Board will
send us. It is not whim or impulse that has decided me but a care-
ful, prayerful, earnest consideration of the whole matter."[43]

Ever the organizer and planner, William gave Anne seven
reasons why he preferred Brazil as a mission site over work in
Burma or Japan:

1. It is just as much in need of a pure Gospel.
2. The vastness of the field—ten million souls without the
   light.

3. It is more healthy than India, and just as healthy as Japan.
4. The race is Caucasian.
5. The language is easier acquired.
6. The Government is more favorable to Evangelical Christianity, and especially to Southern people.
7. It is nearer home.[44]

William's reflections were based not only on the books he read but also the opinions of A. T. Hawthorne and Z. C. Taylor. Friends and relatives of southerners who had already migrated to Brazil also shared their insights.

Each of William's reasons for choosing Brazil was, at best, only partially true. The Catholics in Brazil and America would soon criticize Southern Baptist mission efforts and question whether the Bagbys brought a pure gospel at all. Vast throngs of people in Brazil lived in rural areas that were only accessible by boat or pack mule, making evangelization difficult, if not impossible. Malaria and yellow fever visited the overcrowded cities on the coast seasonally and decimated up to one-third of the inhabitants at times. There were many Caucasians, but most of the population was of African descent or racially mixed. Missionaries acquired the language with ease, but immigration produced settlements of Russians, Irish, Germans, and other Europeans, all speaking their own dialects. The government was favorable to Christianity, but did not allow Protestant meetings in public, and the Catholic church openly persecuted the new evangelicals. They would be nearer home, but letters still took three months by steamer to reach loved ones, and that long period led to an acute sense of separation and loneliness.

William's commitment to missionary service coincided with greater results in his revival services. At Howth Station, twenty-five people asked for prayer and one professed conversion. Relieved, William wrote Anne, "I had feared that the Summer might pass, and I would have no 'golden sheaves' to present to God."[45] William then traveled to First Baptist Church, Corsicana, where fifteen received Christ as Savior. Will so impressed the deacons and church that they wrote him requesting he pastor at Corsicana until the board appointed him to Brazil.[46] He accepted their invitation. The following week he preached at First

Baptist Church, Waco, at the petition of Hawthorne and Carroll. When the revivalist at a meeting in Greenwood became ill, William accepted the invitation to continue that meeting. Twenty-four people professed conversion, and he baptized nineteen at the conclusion of the revival.[47] The interest in Brazil was electrifying. "Everybody I meet is inquiring about Brazil and I am constantly meeting those who have relatives and friends who have been in South America for years," wrote a jubilant William to Anne.[48]

William and Anne were married on October 21, 1880, although Anne had asked that the wedding be postponed until they knew for sure when they were going to Brazil. She feared waiting months or even years in Texas for their application to go through.[49] Anne's father and William Carey Crane performed the ceremony in the Baylor College chapel.[50]

THE FOURTH ATTEMPT

Finding financial support for the young couple was Hawthorne's next concern. The Foreign Mission Board had only recently begun to recover from a turbulent, perilous economic time during the Civil War. At that time the board had thirty missionaries and raised only $50,000 a year for missions. There was a justified reluctance to start a new work with such limited funds.[51] Hawthorne believed Texas to be a vast untapped financial reservoir and began to solicit funds by two methods: Anne Luther Mite Societies and associational preaching tours.

First, Hawthorne capitalized on Anne's influence among Baptist women in Texas to raise financial support for her. Anne had played a major role in the formation of the Southern Baptist W.M.U. in Texas while at Baylor College for Women. William Carey Crane, pastor of First Baptist Church, Independence, strongly advocated "women banding together for religious causes."[52] At his request, the women of his church formed a central committee for missions in 1879. Fannie Breedlove Davis was elected president and Anne Luther corresponding secretary. Both worked hard to organize a statewide mission meeting for women, addressing by hand hundreds of invitations to the event.

Women from all over Texas gathered at First Baptist Church, Austin, during the state convention in October 1880, representing twelve mission societies. While the men appointed Anne as a missionary in the sanctuary of the church, the women elected Fannie Breedlove Davis as president of the newly formed Woman's Missionary Union of Texas in the basement below.[53] Their first item of business was to guarantee financial support for Anne Luther on the mission field.[54] Anne Luther's "offering of herself to Brazil focused the interest of Texas women on Foreign Missions as no other single event had done. It gave purpose and enthusiasm to the W.M.U."[55]

Within a year after Anne Luther Bagby's departure to Brazil, 345 Anne Luther societies had sprung up in the state of Texas. Giving records from Texas state conventions tell a remarkable story of sacrifice and devotion to the mission cause. The societies gave $1,477.06 at Galveston in 1881, $3,044.40 at Belton in 1882, $6,505.20 at San Antonio in 1883, $9,700.24 at Belton in 1888, and $19,224.44 at Waco in 1891. When Anne Bagby spoke at the convention held in Belton in 1892, 107 Anne Luther societies reported, and they had raised a total of $18,315 for her support.[56]

The Anne Luther societies employed several means to solicit funds. Monthly dues were ten cents. The women held ice cream parties and lawn festivals in the summertime. Oyster suppers furthered the cause in the winter months. Quilt squares, embroidered with one's name, sold for ten cents a piece. Baptist women in Texas guaranteed Anne Bagby's yearly salary of $600, and each Anne Luther society tried to raise five dollars each month to do their part.[57]

A. T. Hawthorne and B. H. Carroll divided the Baptist associations of Texas between themselves and went on an extended preaching tour to raise funds.[58] William accompanied both men, as his schedule allowed, speaking at association meetings in Waco, Independence, Union, Bremond, and Galveston.[59] In July of 1880 William spoke at the General Association of Texas at Ennis about Brazil and was guaranteed support. The Texas State Convention voted to do the same for Anne Luther in October.

In November 1880 Will received a letter from Richmond, Virginia, asking him to come and be examined for missionary service by the Foreign Mission Board of the Southern Baptists.[60] He had served the Corsicana church for only a few months, but during that time he had examined a young man for baptism named E. Y. Mullins. Anne and William left Corsicana for Richmond on December 7, 1880. Anne's mother and father were at the train station with most of the church members. At that point, Anne had never met William's father or mother. Anne whispered, "My heart nearly breaks sometimes when I think of the long distance that will soon exist between us and those we love best on earth."[61]

The couple stopped in Missouri on their way to Richmond and stayed with Annie Armstrong and her husband. Anne and Annie particularly enjoyed the visit because they had been childhood playmates. As they continued their journey aboard the train, they sat by ten Indian chiefs traveling to see the president of the United States. "They were dressed in long beaded red blankets, huge fur caps, and had tomahawks for pipes."[62]

William passed his foreign missions examination on December 23, 1880, and requested appointment to Brazil. The board wished to send them to China, but the Bagbys responded that they would go to Brazil even without the board's financial help. The board yielded, and on January 1, 1881, after a week of sightseeing in Washington, D.C., the Bagbys made preparations to set sail for Rio de Janeiro, Brazil.

The Bagbys spent their last Sunday before their departure to Brazil at the Eutaw Place Baptist Church in Richmond, Virginia. Dr. T. P. Graves, missionary from China, gave a lecture on his work in the Orient. William followed with a short talk on Brazil.[63] The next day, they boarded the bark, *Yamyoden,* confident of their mission and sponsorship. Dr. Graves also boarded the *Yamyoden* and offered prayer with the couple. Will wrote that, "Southern Texas is coming nobly to Brazilian interests. The Board is encouraged, and we hope that ere many years earnest workers will be sent out to help us in that land of dark shadows and bright promises."[64] After standing in the harbor for another week, the ship left for Brazil, carrying the hopes and dreams of Texas Baptists. It was a step of faith like many the Bagbys would take in the coming years. They were subsidized mainly by Texas Baptists, and they had raised only enough funds for three months thus far.[65]

ABOARD THE *YAMYODEN*

Anne recorded the voyage from Chesapeake Bay to Rio de Janeiro in a small diary. Seasickness was the first trial the young couple faced. William suffered from it throughout the forty-eight-day voyage. At first, they attempted to sleep in separate cabins during the night so Anne could rest, but this plan was quickly discarded. She noted, "Never mean to let Mr. B. spend another night from me because of sickness unless it be absolutely necessary. I imagined that he died in the night and 'they' were putting him over board before morning so that I might not have the grief of seeing it done."[66] Not all of Anne's dreams were so diabolical. Her father and mother, sister and brother, and various relatives all frequented her dreams. She beamed, saying, "What kind fortune to be permitted thus to spend a portion of each night at home."[67]

During the voyage, Anne also discovered with great joy that she and William were about to start their own family. Anne often wondered if she was seasick or merely experiencing the sickness that often accompanied pregnancy. In spite of the good news of a new family, Anne struggled consistently with homesickness throughout the journey. These feelings only intensified after her departure. Anne wrote her mother, "Mr. B. kisses me sometimes for you and Pa when I am homesick and to cheer me tells me that you have each other to lean upon and that he has only me."[68]

In spite of seasickness and homesickness, William and Anne relished the trip to Rio de Janeiro. They were the only passengers on the ship and talked often with the captain, a boisterous sailor weighing more than 300 pounds. Most of their time was spent in study, and William fished occasionally. Sundays were spent reading the Bible and singing hymns in their private room upon the request of the indifferent captain. Anne reported to her parents, "We have been able to read a great deal—to reflect a great deal—to pray a great deal."[69]

Upon sighting the coastline of Brazil, Anne shared, "Mr. B. is so joyful to the approach of land that he finds it difficult to control himself. He has given way to many little indignities and demonstrations of his joy."[70]

The view was breathtaking as the Bagbys arrived in the Bay

of Rio on the afternoon of March 2, 1881. Anne reported, "Really I never saw such beauty in my life before! I could hardly believe that so much grandeur of scenery could be concentrated . . . And yet all this loveliness is merely a mask—back of it there is sin—sin and not light at all."[71] The Bagbys quickly telegraphed Tupper in Richmond upon their arrival. He, in turn, telephoned Independence, informing Anne's parents of the missionary couple's safe arrival. The response by those at Baylor College for Women was spontaneous and ecstatic.

Chapter 3

Preparation for Ministry: Santa Barbara, Sao Paulo

My highest aspiration, Pa is to lead the life my Mother leads . . . Mr. Bagby is truly a good, as well as a talented man. I am perfectly happy as his wife. I would not have him change in any way. He will grow, I know, but it is all he could be 'for his age' . . . I doubt whether he will ever feel able to leave his field of labor to return even for a visit to his native land . . . When I think of how very short life is in comparison to eternity I am willing to toil on patiently. . . .
—Anne to Father, May 21, 1881[1]

LAND OF THE SOUTHERN CROSS

It took three months to get from Texas to Brazil, but it would take Will and Anne far longer to adapt to the culture of their new home. Their knowledge of Brazil had come mainly through talks with Z. C. Taylor and A. T. Hawthorne. Brazil, like the United States, had a rich history filled with colorful personalities and notable events.

Pedro Alvares Cabral discovered Brazil in April 1500. He designated it as "The Land of the Southern Cross" because of four large stars, three of the first magnitude, that lit up the evening sky. Subsequent merchants began to call the country "Brazil" because of the large population of fire-red trees in the area called brazilwood. Portugal was slow to colonize the region but did send out an exploratory expedition in 1501 headed by Gaspar de Lemos. Amerigo Vespucci was the scribe of their efforts, and Europeans later gave his name to the continent.[2]

27

When the threat of French capture of Brazil became real in 1532, the Portuguese crown quickly decided to develop the new area and establish a feudal system of captaincies. The government assigned sections of land to individual colonists who could pass them onto their heirs. A more centralized plan replaced the land grant system when it foundered in 1548, but large plantations and slavery had already become a permanent characteristic of the Portuguese colony. This facet of Brazilian life was much like that of the Old South in the United States.[3]

Immigration patterns in Brazil led to a racially mixed population. Many early Brazilian colonists were deported Portuguese criminals who were given another chance in the New World. They intermarried with the Indian population, creating a large population of mulattoes. Other settlers included Jews who fled persecution in Portugal and sought refuge in a less hostile environment. Population figures for the year 1600 showed little colonization after one century, however. Total inhabitants were estimated to be "57,000: 25,000 whites, 18,000 Indians, and 14,000 Africans."[4]

Foreign trade launched the move toward Brazilian independence from Portugal. When Napoleon invaded Portugal in 1806, the royal family fled to Brazil under the naval protection of Britain. Dom Juan, deported regent of Portugal, quickly decreed Brazil's ports open to trade with all nations not at war with the Portuguese crown. He also revoked the decree against the development of manufacturing in Brazil. In 1815 Dom Juan formally recognized Brazil as an equal partner in the "United Kingdom of Portugal, Brazil, and Algarve."[5]

When Dom Juan returned to Portugal because of political unrest in 1821, he left Dom Pedro, his son, in authority. Dom Juan recommended that his son take leadership of any movement to give Brazil independence if government leaders in Portugal attempted to reestablish Brazil as a colony. Following his father's advice, Dom Pedro proclaimed Brazilian independence on September 7, 1822. He ratified a new constitution on March 5, 1824, which created a lower house of the legislature and established Roman Catholicism as the state religion.[6]

Political mistakes and accusations of despotism led to Dom Pedro's abdication in 1831. The legislature appointed his five-

year-old son, Dom Pedro II, as legatee. After nine years of tur-
moil, political leaders agreed to advance the age of the heir-des-
ignate, and crowned Dom Pedro II emperor in 1841. A wise
political leader, he reigned until 1889.[7]

Many considered the reign of Dom Pedro II as the "Golden
Age of Brazilian history."[8] Sugar, tobacco, cotton, leather, rub-
ber, and coffee exports grew exponentially throughout his administration. Coffee exports, for example, increased from an average of 19,000 tons in the 1820s to 58,000 tons in the 1830s;
100,000 tons in the 1840s; and 158,000 tons in the 1850s. After
1850, Brazil contributed more than half the world's coffee sup-
ply.[9] The success of coffee on the world market also caused wide
fluctuations in the Brazilian economy, however. The difference
in pennies per pound created wealth or heartache depending
upon the harvest and time of year. Money in Brazil was unmer-
cifully inconsistent.[10]

Dom Pedro II began to encourage immigration and tech-
nology to offset the labor shortage. European immigrants
surged into the coffee-producing areas, especially the province
of Sao Paulo. In fact, 90,000 European immigrants came to Sao
Paulo in 1887 alone.[11] Brazil began to develop a new railroad
and telegraph system underwritten by North American and west
European companies. Investors speculated on electric lighting,
municipal tramways, and the adaptation of steam power and
electricity to shipping and manufacturing.[12]

One result of Dom Pedro II's policies was a kind of religious
pluralism like that of the United States. The sheer number of
people pouring in from different nationalities and religious
backgrounds began to dismantle the authority of the Roman
Catholic church in Brazil. It was in this setting that Will and
Anne began to proclaim the Baptist way of life.

WORK AMONG THE AMERICANS

Will and Anne stayed aboard the *Yamyoden* in Rio Bay because of rumors of a yellow fever epidemic. After doctors as-
sured them that the reports were false, the couple disembarked
and lodged in Carson's Hotel until travel plans for Santa Bar-

bara could be developed. Two American dentists helped William and introduced him to many men in the city.[13] A former Confederate soldier brought a letter of welcome from Mrs. Ellis of Santa Barbara, and a few days later the Bagbys traveled by train to their new mission site in Sao Paulo state.[14] A gentleman who brought a slave to carry their luggage greeted them at the Sao Paulo station, and they proceeded on horseback to Mrs. Ellis' home. William commented to his mother in a letter, "It seems very strange to be again in a land where slavery is the social condition of the Negro race."[15]

William arranged a meeting with E. H. Quillen, the Baptist pastor at Santa Barbara, and began to evaluate the strength of the mission. Quillen had written the Foreign Mission Board several times with glowing reports of the field, promising that, "ministers would find no difficulty in taking care of themselves after the first year."[16] William quickly wrote Tupper asserting that this was not so at all. The future of the church at Santa Barbara, in fact, looked dismal due to leadership conflicts within the church and the moral degeneracy of the American population.

Leadership problems involved E. H. Quillen and Alfonso Teixeira de Albuquerque, a recently converted priest. Both men traveled to Piriciba to start a school, but they came home after its failure, harboring an intense animosity toward each other. Quillen accused Teixeira of getting drunk and entertaining prostitutes while in Piriciba. Teixeira claimed that he only did what he saw Quillen do.[17] The issue split the church. So the small group of Baptists were divided, some meeting at the original building, and others meeting at the "Station church."

It soon became evident to Bagby that Quillen was not fit to minister to the Santa Barbara colony and would be of little help in the work.[18] Neither the Americans nor the Brazilians held Quillen in high regard. Bagby wrote the board, "There are three Baptist preachers in this region, but one of them has become a spiritualist, and another scarcely ever preaches. We need pious and earnest men!"[19] Within a month after the Bagbys arrival, Quillen resigned and asked Bagby to take charge of the mission.[20]

The spiritual difficulties that plagued the Santa Barbara church were symptomatic of moral problems found throughout the colony. Anne wrote, "The Americans, as a colony, have done great injury to the mission cause. Only a few Christians have kept the light burning in this dark valley."[21] Anne was mortified at the gossip, backbiting, and lack of regard for the Sabbath among the colonists.[22] She also learned quickly that ugly rumors about her and Will could travel to Texas through letters written by meanspirited churchgoers.[23] She lamented, "No longer am I, dear Ma and Pa, an infant in your strong arms as I have so often since wished myself to be, but I am a woman, a married woman, a missionary far away from you in a strange land!"[24] She hoped the conversion of General Hawthorne would provide a "strong argument for Christianity" among the immigrants.[25]

The Bagbys decided to study Portuguese at the *Internacional de Campinas,* a Presbyterian school at Campinas, thirty miles from Santa Barbara. Their teacher was a Brazilian who had attended college in the United States for several years and spoke English and Portuguese.[26] The school had recently lost half its faculty due to a conflict over the proper role of education and evangelism in mission work. The more evangelistic side had prevailed.[27]

After seven months of study, William and Anne took charge of the *Internacional de Campinas* when Nannie Henderson, Anne's closest friend and matron of the school, was forced to vacation at Santos due to physical and emotional exhaustion.[28] William was already teaching an arithmetic class in Portuguese, but now instructed six additional classes in Portuguese and one in English. He gave all instruction and explanations in Portuguese, thus aiding him in the study of the language.[29] Anne listened to several students recite in English and Portuguese each day and led a music class.[30] The first time she whipped a boy's hand with a ruler, however, she suffered a headache and trembled the rest of the evening.[31]

In the midst of his studies, William began to repair the troubled church at Santa Barbara. He held a revival meeting in June 1881, and six colonists professed conversion. He helped the Station church reunite with the Santa Barbara church a short time later. Although William only preached at the Santa Barbara church two Sundays a month, the church began to grow spiritually and renew its commitment to reach Brazil for Christ.[32]

Will attended services at the Presbyterian mission the other two Sundays out of the month. Both he and Anne believed this would facilitate their mastery of Portuguese. After a few months, both could sing in Portuguese, and William could speak fluently enough to buy items from the Brazilian market.[33]

In September 1881 William attended the general meeting of Presbyterians in Sao Paulo City and returned excited; he had conversed with several missionaries who had been on the field for nearly twenty years. The fellowship with fellow evangelicals was inspiring, but William continued to write Hawthorne and Tupper pleading for them to send Southern Baptist reinforcements to Brazil.[34] He lamented, "Oh, that God would impress many more to come to this vast moral charnel house! The priesthood is rotten to the core, the masses of people are buried in superstition and immorality. Materialism, skepticism, atheism and rationalism are rife. . . ."[35] A. T. Hawthorne contacted Z. C. Taylor and convinced him to cease his studies at Louisville, get married, and set out for Brazil to help the Bagbys. Taylor accepted the challenge and returned to Texas to help Hawthorne raise money for his support. Shortly afterward, Hawthorne performed the wedding ceremony of Z. C. Taylor and Kate Crawford. The Taylors arrived in Rio de Janeiro on February 13, 1882.[36]

The two couples officially organized into the Brazilian Baptist Mission on March 17, 1882. Bagby and Taylor held a revival meeting at the Santa Barbara church in April 1882, in which eleven professed conversion and five were baptized. At this time William could preach four sermons in Portuguese by reading from a manuscript.[37]

Z. C. Taylor made an immediate impact on the mission field. He preached twenty-five times to the Americans and once through an interpreter to the Brazilians in his first three months on the field. He maintained that Southern Baptists gave "a new impulse to other missions by our strenuous efforts to give the gospel to Americans and Brazilians."[38] Bagby continued to preach in homes at the request of local Brazilians, sometimes speaking to fifty eager people.[39]

Soon the men began to face persecution from other missionaries. Taylor wrote Hawthorne, "The Presbyterians here are stiff and cold and strict. Some of them I fear have missed their calling: especially some of the wives."[40]

The work of a missionary's wife on the field could leave one cold and stiff, however. Balancing being a wife, mother and missionary often left Anne despondent and depressed. The fact that the missionaries had not established a permanent mission site troubled her. Busy teaching and learning the language, she confided to the Anne Luther Societies in Missouri that, "I have not felt myself to be any more of a missionary, in one sense of the word, than when at home."[41] She wrote her parents that, "A good part of my work must be silent watching. I see that. I am fully content with my calling. I shall always find plenty to do. I want to hold the position Ma holds—matron of a boarding school—when we establish a mission."[42] A few months later she added:

> I am a woman now and I must find the strength that lies in me individually, not that which comes from my surroundings or from those who reared me, that I may be able to be of service to others. I must not be "enjoying" all the time, I must be "enjoyed." I know I am becoming stronger and yet I feel so weak at times that I think I must give up altogether.[43]

Anne and Kate formulated plans to start a "poor school" and wrote churches in Texas and Missouri for support. The board, however, requested they suspend their efforts until the future. Frustrated, the women decided their chief ministry would be reading the Bible in the homes of the native women. They insisted, "Any woman can leave home for a few hours a day, can she not, who is in good health and has healthy babies?"[44]

DON'T DESPISE THE DAY OF SMALL THINGS

The condition of the mission at Santa Barbara had disappointed the Bagbys when they arrived in Brazil. E. H. Quillen's reports to the Foreign Mission Board were much like the fraudulent propaganda that Brazilian pamphleteers produced to tempt southerners to migrate to their country. Quillen's alcoholism and drug addiction offered little hope of spiritual camaraderie for the new missionaries.[45] The only Brazilian whom they had converted, Teixeira, left the church with a deep animosity toward Americans because of Quillen. Finally, the Santa

Barbara church, though improving spiritually under the leadership of Bagby and Taylor, did not have the heart of an Antioch
church to reach the surrounding cities. However disillusioned,
the Bagbys early years had given them the strength of character,
vision, and call of God to persevere.

From his earliest memories, Will had aspirations to be a
preacher, much to his mother's delight and influence. His pietis-
tic home, the visiting frontier evangelists, and the unfulfilled
ambition of his sister to become a missionary created soil which
made him ready for missionary service. His early experiences as
a schoolteacher, editor of a newspaper, and revivalist were merely transplanted to foreign ground and became his missionary
strategy for Brazil.

Anne also brought a rich heritage to Brazil. She received exceptional training compared to most of the women of her time.
Her experiences at Baylor College for Women as matron of the
boarding school, professor, and gifted musician would all be
used in Brazil. Anne had an earthy side too, however. From
available evidence, it appears that Anne was headstrong and
even spoiled, sometimes throwing temper tantrums that would
last several days. Much of Anne's initial interest in missions may
have been an unconscious response to her father's unfulfilled
dreams of becoming a missionary.

To their credit, Will and Anne possessed a fiery, entrepre-
neurial spirit and were willing to fight for what they believed. To
be successful in Brazil would demand nothing less. The Bagbys
hard-fisted approach to the board's request to send them to
China was certainly not the last time that tension would enter
that relationship. Indeed, the relationship between the Bagbys
and the Foreign Mission Board would become very tenuous, very
soon. Their arrival in Santa Barbara marked the beginning of
fruitful Southern Baptist work in Brazil.

The Bagbys represented the first successful foreign mission
attempt of Southern Baptists in Brazil. However, they did not
work alone. The role of Z. C. Taylor and A. T. Hawthorne in the
establishment of the greatest mission field of the Southern Baptist Convention should not be minimized.

In many ways Z. C. Taylor had laid the spiritual foundation
for Brazilian missions with his vision many years before. After

meeting with Tupper in 1878, he prepared for mission work in Brazil. His studies at Baylor College for Men and Southern Seminary were based on a plan of action set out by the corresponding secretary of the Foreign Mission Board. Richard Ratcliff, former pastor of the Santa Barbara church, reaffirmed this plan during a missionary emphasis conference at Baylor.[46] Taylor invited him to speak at the meeting and housed him for the entire week so he could learn more about Brazil. The primary obstacle that prevented Taylor from being the first successful Southern Baptist missionary sent to Brazil was the financial condition of the board. To a great extent, the Anne Luther societies and the mystique of the female missionary had provided the funds for the Bagbys to reach the promised land first.

A. T. Hawthorne's efforts removed the remaining roadblock of monetary support and set the financial foundation for great success in Brazil. He wrote Anne: "From the night on which I first mentioned this subject to you . . . I have labored and prayed for the success of this mission, as I have never before labored for any other cause."[47] Hawthorne was not stretching the truth. Southern Baptists surely would have entered the continent at some point in time, but Hawthorne's fervent pleas and financial prowess put the missionaries in the midst of an emerging country. Brazil was eager to change and ready to accept Protestant viewpoints. Will and Anne Bagby reached the field at a propitious time.

After several months of ministry together, Bagby and Taylor discarded Santa Barbara as an acceptable mission site, and decided to take a railroad tour through Brazil to discover a more suitable location. They traveled through the empire and chose Salvador, Bahia, as the best location. They wrote the board, citing five reasons for their choice:

1. In this county all the large cities are on the seaboard. They are the centers of national and provincial life, commercially, industrially, socially, and religiously. Our work ought to commence in some center—some point of radiation.
2. In a large coast city we can reach the thousands together while in the interior the people are scattered over a vast area.

3. In a coast city we would have business advantages which we could not secure away from the coast.
4. On the coast we would be in direct communication with the Board and with our home work.
5. If the work is commenced in a large city we not only can reach the thousands at once and together but a footing gained there will give us prestige elsewhere.[48]

Their correspondence failed to mention the fact that A. T. Hawthorne and several evangelical missionaries in Brazil had recommended strongly that they settle in Rio de Janeiro first.[49]

Bagby and Taylor visited Teixeira in Piriciba and asked the ex-priest to join them as the Portuguese teacher in the Bahia mission. He accepted. The Santa Barbara church had restored Teixeira when he confessed to some wrongdoing during his trip with Quillen, but he vehemently denied any immorality. Bagby and Taylor considered him extremely competent except in his financial dealings. Consequently, they requested he sign a one-year teaching contract with several stipulations: no other line of work, no debts without Bagby and Taylor's consent, and a correct Christian lifestyle.[50] Taylor wrote Hawthorne, "If he proves faithful, we hope to recommend him to the Board for appointment as a missionary."[51]

The three families set sail for Salvador, Bahia, on August 24, 1882, and arrived a week later. The entourage included twelve individuals: William and Anne Bagby, their daughter Ermine, Z. C. and Kate Taylor, Teixeira and his wife, their four children, and a young servant girl named Mary.[52]

Within eighteen months of the Bagbys' arrival in Brazil, they had restored spiritual vitality to the Santa Barbara church, cultivated friendships with other missionaries, and developed a strategic plan for the future of Baptist work in Brazil. The influence of the Bagbys and their comrades in Brazil was imperceptible at first, but their accomplishments at Santa Barbara were the fountainhead for all that would follow.

Chapter 4

A Foundation for Ministry: Salvador, Bahia

Last night . . . Mr. Bagby, myself and Ermine, Sr. Teixeira and his little son, took the street car near our house and went out to meet two women who were candidates for baptism. When we left the car we noticed that we were not unobserved and, as we neared the water, we saw that we were in quite a crowd of rowdyish boys and men.

Mr. Bagby seemed to be intuitively on his guard; he said he didn't want a crowd, the place being a strange one and the people especially ignorant and superstitious; but I told him I anticipated no trouble. He was thinking especially of the noise that such fellows sometimes make at our baptisms, rather than of violence. However, we women stepped aside and were just about arranging the sheets into a kind of tent to screen us from view—though it was almost if not quite dark, there being little or no moonlight—when we were startled by an uproar among the men, one voice above all calling down vengeance upon these heretics who couldn't be satisfied with worshiping in their houses, but must choose public places on the beach even for their worship, which they should know was against the law. Such a coarse angry voice it was, and such a noise accompanying it! I didn't know what to make of it—why Mr. Bagby didn't come to tell me there was no need of alarm or to give me a few words of explanation.

. . . I took Ermine in my arms and waited—not, however, very much troubled, thinking it was a drunken man whom the office was arresting.

When Mr. Bagby appeared, I asked no questions, simply followed him, as he said there would be no baptism that night. When I found a good opportunity, after the women were sent home . . . and the noise had

37

almost ceased, I ventured to ask Mr. Bagby, "Tell me, what is all this noise about?"

"Nothing," he said, "simply that I am a prisoner."

— Anne to Parents[1]

BEGINNING A NEW WORK

The Bagbys, Taylors, and Teixeiras had difficulty finding adequate housing in Salvador, Bahia, after their arrival and had to settle for a small house in the suburbs. Each family had one room, and everyone shared a hall, kitchen, and dining room. Anne and Kate supervised the housekeeping, rotating weekly. Due to a lack of funds, the missionaries made furniture out of pine boxes covered with dark cloth, as well as wardrobes, wash stands, and book cases. They also decided not to organize into a church body until they could find a better mission location in the city.[2]

The Presbyterian mission welcomed the new missionaries to Salvador and invited Bagby to preach in their services. He filled the pulpit three times within two weeks of his arrival in the city. The church was small, with only twenty-five members, but Bagby characterized them as faithful and zealous. He delivered his sermons in Portuguese and remarked to his mother in a letter, "I can now speak Portuguese somewhat plainly and easily and so feel greatly encouraged."[3] Bagby's fourth quarter report for 1882 revealed that he preached twelve sermons—six in the Presbyterian chapel and six in the Baptist church.[4]

In spite of a significant increase in foreign missions giving by Texans in the decade of the 1880s, the Bagbys faced a severe deficiency of funds during their first years in Brazil. They received only one letter from the board the first twelve months they were in Brazil. Writing to Tupper, Will exclaimed, "Am much afraid letters have been lost. As I have not received last quarter's salary yet, I am likely to be seriously in need before our next month's mail."[5] Anne revealed to her parents, "We know there are funds in the treasury for us individually and we can not account for their non-reception."[6] Will wrote Hawthorne: "Have not heard from Dr. Tupper since his letter of six months ago, and we cannot imagine the reason. Had it not been for some money I got from our brethren at Santa Barbara, I would have been without any money whatever."[7]

A draft of $145 came late in January 1882 and partially relieved the couple's financial distress, but the promised drafts from previous quarters were never forthcoming.[8] The Bagbys began to believe their own board had abandoned them.

The Foreign Mission Board refused to support Teixeira and his family until he proved faithful to the task, so the missionary couples paid for Teixeira's housing and salary out of their personal funds. The board's inaction was based on a letter they had received from Methodist missionary J. J. Ransom:

> I am personally acquainted with Antonio Teixeira de Albuquerque, ex-priest. I took him up in Rio de Janeiro where he had no money, no friends, and scant clothing for himself and family. He cost me personally, first and last, about $300, and I expended on him more than three times that amount from donations of friends and funds of my Mission. The Presbyterians laughed at me all the while, but I was confident that I would make a grand success of the man, that is, a flaming reformer and a good Methodist. When I cut down his wages, Teixeira withdrew, protesting he "would always be a Methodist." But shortly after I heard that Mr. Quillen had put him under the water, and all the Baptists were rejoiced when Teixeira told them "he had been a Baptist all the while, only he had not met the Baptists" . . . If Mr. Quillen has converted Teixeira, or can convert him, or if bro. Bagby can do that, you may congratulate yourselves on the acquisition, otherwise I fear your gain is a small one . . .[9]

Will wrote his brother, "We believe we will be more than repaid in the future by the good he will do."[10] His assessment of Teixeira's integrity proved to be accurate. The fact that Teixeira's family spoke little English also challenged the missionaries to learn Portuguese more quickly in order to communicate.[11]

A lack of financial support from the Foreign Mission Board proved to be a significant setback to the work. A letter from Tupper in October 1882 included only a small gift from B. H. Carroll. Bagby responded, "We are among strangers, and enemies to the gospel and are almost entirely without means of subsistence."[12] Bagby wrote the board in desperation: "We have not yet heard anything from you and know not why our remittances have not reached us. . . . We would long ago have suffered for the necessaries of life had it not been for the kindness of some friends, and we are still without means of our own!"[13] The American consul, a widower, spent many nights eating and sharing with the missionaries and lent them money during troubled times. He, in fact, saved the Baptist mission from ruin with his financial support.[14]

After three months, the families moved into a large house in the center of Salvador. The house was a former baron's home converted into a Jesuit school and contained thirty rooms and a large meeting hall.[15] Annual rent was $750, and Anne wrote her father saying, "You would have no trouble whatever in seeing your girls away if you had this house."[16] She requested that he not tell anyone of their new "palace," fearing jealousy at home. The families occupied the second and third floors, while the rooms on the first floor were used for a book deposit, school room, and large assembly hall that could hold 200 people.[17]

Having secured better housing arrangements, they organized the First Baptist Church of Brazil on October 15, 1882. Members included William and Anne Bagby, Z. C. and Kate Taylor, and Teixeira. Although Teixeira was the only national member, it was the first church that could properly be called Brazilian: "It took a Portuguese name, *Primeira Igreja Batista,* its services were held in Portuguese, and its goal was to develop a national membership. The missionaries had prepared themselves linguistically, they had left the familiar surroundings of the Santa Barbara American community, and they had abandoned their task of chaplaincy to foreign emigres."[18] The foundation for Southern Baptist mission work in Brazil was established.

Two months after settling into their new home, the missionaries began to concentrate on furnishing the preaching hall. Will wrote, "Oh! for the day when the holiness and peace of the Gospel shall illumine this abyss of shame and misery! . . . We have been preaching every Sunday for our households, but could not invite the public because we have not yet arranged seats."[19] They purchased several benches, and began two worship services on Sundays. Other services during the week included a prayer meeting Wednesday night and a song practice Friday night.[20] Attendance by the end of February reached more than sixty, and the two missionary couples began a weekly mission meeting to talk about the work and discuss future plans.[21] Z. C. Taylor wrote:

> Senhor [sic] Teixeira occupied the pulpit at night, when our congregations were larger. Brother Bagby and I would occupy, one the inner and the other the outer door of the first two halls, conducting attendants to the farthest preaching hall. The inner man was to maintain order, the other to give the welcome, hand out tracts, and invite them to return.
>
> Day by day the study of the language was the main thing for awhile. Gradually we began to visit the homes of those who attended. However, in three months priestly opposition and a wane in public curiosity left us an empty house. One Sunday morning there were present at public service only our three families.
>
> Monday mornings we missionaries had our special meetings for prayer and counsel. The morning following that low Sunday the subject was how to get the gospel to the people. They had failed to come to us. We must go to them. We then agreed to slip a New Testament into our pocket and go out into the streets, into their shops, anywhere we could get one or more to hear. We interested many in this way, and little by little our hall began to fill again. This taught us a lesson just when we needed it: that the people were to be saved as individuals, not en masse. . . .[22]

The women quickly organized a small school to teach the Bible and English to women and children.[23] Anne was deeply concerned for the conversion of her pupils. She wrote Hawthorne, "I think the Presbyterians err principally in placing too much force upon educating and too little upon the work of the Spirit." She said further, "School work must grow out of the spreading of the gospel—it should not precede it."[24] Anne's pregnancy with their second child, however, limited her missionary efforts.[25]

Anne Bagby discovered a vast difference between her efforts at teaching the "colored" Sunday School at home and actually living among people of another race. The adjustment to Brazilian culture was difficult. She wrote to her mother saying, "House-

keeping is almost unendurable work here with foreigners, especially with careless cooks and little money."[26] Anne complained
later, "I get very blue sometimes. It is a wretchedly ugly part of
the city to live in—so bad for going out walking—so public and
dirty are the streets for four or five blocks around us."[27] She
wrote her sister Zollie, "We live in a noisy part of the city with an
innumerable number of Negroes in all the lower stories, oh,
there is unheard trouble!"[28] She shared with her father:

> We are surely living in the central part of the city, judging by
> the people that pass on the street and the number of fights that
> go on. . . . One night after worship, a man who had stabbed
> another rushed through our front door and tried to get
> upstairs, but, seeing people above, broke open a door that led
> downstairs into the backyard, and thus escaped the police.[29]

Anne was frightened because she could "feel" foreign eyes gaz-
ing at her anytime she left the house.[30] In a land where whites,
blacks, and mulattoes shared social equality, Anne discovered
prejudices that surprised her.[31]

METHODS AND STRATEGIES

Bagby and Taylor had little theological training and were
dependent on the biblical record for their methods as a result.
Taylor commented, "We could not lean on our own understand-
ings, but had to appeal to God and the Book. I read the whole
of the Acts to find out where the Apostles preached."[32] The apostles preached mainly in the cities, so the missionaries decided
they would also concentrate their efforts in the urban areas.

Both men had witnessed the development of pioneer Baptist work while growing up in Texas. Their experiences in Brazil
would approximate roughly what had happened in their home
state. Indeed, the early South American missions may be con-
ceived of as an extension of the American frontier. There was little difference between the Methodist circuit rider evangelizing
America and "the Protestant missionary who endeavored to
spread the gospel throughout the immense hinterland of Brazil
where horse and mule were the sole means of transportation."[33]

Protestantism conquered the "wild west" of the United States and would do the same in Brazil.

Bagby and Taylor quickly found that the simple evangelistic service they experienced on the Texas frontier appealed to the Brazilians as well. The Brazilians responded to a "plain and unornamented Church, clergy without robes, and services based on experiencing the vital truths of salvation and Christian growth . . . where ritual and formalism were reduced to the barest minimum."[34] This style was a direct response to the empty liturgy and elaborate processions promoted by the Roman Catholic Church. Though the services were simple, the Baptist missionaries often preached for several hours. One new female missionary on the field reported hearing Z. C. Taylor preach for three hours and not understanding a word he said.[35]

At the end of a service, the preacher would ask if any had made a decision for Christ. Invitations were never open to the public. The missionary would ask for a show of hands, would note those who raised their hands, and visit them during the week. After counseling with the interested and ascertaining the validity of their commitment, the missionary would introduce the seeker to the church and begin the process of becoming a member.[36]

Membership in the Baptist church in Salvador, Bahia, required a public meeting of all the members of the church. Bagby or Taylor usually served as moderator and examined potential church members. Some questions included:

> When did you first hear the gospel? What effect did it have upon you? Do you now believe in Jesus? Did you always believe in Him? Here he would or would not make a distinction between a historical and a saving faith. Has your heart changed? In what way? Are you sure your heart is changed or is it just your mind? Have you any enemies? Do you owe any debts? . . . Are you willing to pay them, beginning now to pay them off as fast as you can? Do you work on Sundays? . . . Have you told anybody about Jesus yet? Are you willing to bring all your family and friends into the gospel? . . . Are you willing to pay the tenth or contribute liberally of your possessions and gains according as God prospers you, for the salvation of your fellow man? . . . Are you willing to take these believers as your brethren and sisters, to enjoy with them the blessings of God,

suffer with them, and work with them for the salvation of all the people? . . . Are you married? Is the woman you are living with your lawful wife? . . . Are you ready to make the marriage legal? . . . Are you willing to establish family worship, reading the Bible, singing God's praises, and praying His blessings on your home and loved ones?[37]

After answering these questions satisfactorily, the floor was opened to church members who could then interrogate the candidate. Membership standards were high in the Baptist church, but once accepted, the convert found a new family, a new culture, and a new religion. In an unsettled and changing continent, it is not surprising that many Brazilians found a new sense of identity among the Baptists.[38]

Bagby and Taylor provided a firm foundation for the native church in Brazil by emphasizing tithing and high ethical living. "The principle of tithing was instilled into every heart of each new Christian before he became a member of the church."[39] In fact, a new Christian was not eligible for membership until he showed a correct understanding of biblical giving. This characteristic of Baptist work paved the way for more indigenous work and strong national leadership.[40] Ethical standards were set high by the missionaries in response to the moral decadence they noted around them. As a result, "the use of alcoholic liquors, the use of tobacco, dancing, attendance at theaters or cinemas, the slightest participation in the Carnival" were all considered evils by Brazilian Baptists.[41]

Z. C. Taylor's main strategy was to preach the gospel rather than establish churches or schools.[42] His tactic was to preach in an area several times and allow the church "to spring up spontaneously in the regions evangelized."[43] He feared that Christianity had "set down to build and fortify and lost sight of the main thing, to bring everything into subjection to Christ."[44] Taylor stated: "My mission was to go everywhere, preaching the gospel. For fifteen years, perhaps, there was not on an average of one church a year organized. The main thing was to preach, preach, preach."[45] Taylor's future evangelistic thrust focused on rural towns instead of the larger cities.[46]

William Bagby, on the other hand, believed preaching stations, churches, and schools must be organized in the large cities so that new converts could be built up in their faith and then reach their friends and neighbors.[47] His plan required more time, but proved to be more successful than Z. C. Taylor's concept. Taylor's idea of preaching with little institutional organization made his work too dependent on the personality and drive of the missionary.

Preaching the gospel was not the only method of reaching the masses in Brazil. The earliest work done by Protestants in Brazil had been through the American and British Bible Societies. The societies distributed thousands of copies of the Bible in the homes of Brazilians and worked to improve the Portuguese translation.[48] They sent copies of the scriptures to foreign merchants in the larger cities who distributed them to the public. Most Protestant missionaries also relied on the income they received from selling Bibles, and they enjoyed incredible success in this endeavor.[49] Bible distribution was big business in Brazil, and both Bagby and Taylor benefitted.[50]

Producing and distributing tracts also furthered the Baptist cause. The missionaries wrote and printed several tracts to explain Baptist convictions to the public. Bagby prepared a tract on images, showing them to be idols according to Scripture. Kate Taylor translated a tract entitled, *The Portrait of Mary as She is in Heaven,* which denied the divinity of Jesus' mother, Mary. The Bahia mission published three other tracts in Portuguese: *Bible Doctrines, The Holy Bible on Baptism,* and *A Brief Biblical Catechism.* The missionaries used the catechism in their newly organized Sunday School. The tracts were very effective, and Bagby requested a publishing fund for the mission since no Baptist literature existed in Portuguese other than the works the missionaries had translated.[51]

Along with tracts, the missionaries distributed several translations of books through the mission bookstore. One work was *Ford's History of the Baptists,* a book that Z. C. Taylor translated adding the following sections: *The Declaration of Faith, Parliamentary Practice,* and *Church Covenant and Government of the Local Church.* The book maintained that a "trail of blood" could be traced throughout the centuries and that Baptists were the true heirs of the New Testament church. Taylor beamed, "One ex-canon, Ottoni, said this was the best of all of our books, as it was the only historical proof against Romish innovations."[52]

The greatest single factor contributing to the success of Baptists in Brazil, however, was the effectiveness of native preachers in reaching their own people. Teixeira was but the first in a long line of gifted men who brought salvation to his own people. He led Wednesday night services and attracted many people with "a series of discussions on the leading doctrines of Rome, giving his experiences as a priest."[53] A prominent officer of the government attended the lectures and offered to publish them in the city newspaper. In Teixeira's first article, entitled "The Apostate Priest," he proclaimed, "I apostatized from Rome, but not from Christ!"[54] An editorial war followed that further promoted Baptist views. Bagby noted, "While it has angered the priests, it has opened the eyes of the people, and they are busy pondering its truths."[55]

A strong dependence on native leadership only made sense. Bagby and Taylor had not adequately mastered Portuguese, so they read their sermons from a prepared manuscript. This not only required a great deal of time in preparation, but it resulted in a church service more formalistic than the missionaries wanted.[56] In May 1883 Bagby reported that he had preached nineteen sermons the previous quarter, and he had written them all out in longhand. Teixeira, however, was having "great success preaching, handing out bibles, testaments, and tracts, and scattering invitations to the services throughout the city."[57]

William Bagby and Z. C. Taylor founded the first indigenous Baptist church in Salvador, Bahia. Bagby also began to formulate his strategy for ministry: preaching in large cities, utilizing native helpers, establishing preaching stations, and eventually organizing churches and teaching institutions. The influence of Will and Anne Bagby also extended northward to Texas and guided financial and human resources toward "The Land of the Southern Cross."

THE TEXAS CONNECTION

Anne had wished to leave for Brazil as soon as possible so that the ties between friends and associates would not grow faint. With men like A. T. Hawthorne and B. H. Carroll rallying the foreign mission cause in Texas, however, she had nothing to fear.

William and Anne Bagby represented the starting point of a strong partnership between Texas and Brazilian Baptists, which continues to the present time.

When the Bagbys departed for Brazil, Texas was still considered a home mission state by the Southern Baptist Convention. Growth had been slow but certain. In 1848 the Baptist population numbered 2,000 with seventy-five churches.[58] By 1882 the state convention records showed twenty missionaries on the field, thirty-seven in 1883, thirty-five in 1884, and forty-six in 1885.[59] As a result missionary news from Brazil was much like home missionary articles already found in the Baptist papers circulated in Texas.

Because of the work of A. T. Hawthorne, foreign missions fever swept Texas during the decade of the 1880s. Besides the Bagbys, other Texans like the Z. C. Taylors, the C. D. Daniels, the E. A. Puthuffs, and Mina Everett surrendered for service in Brazil.[60] J. M. Carroll, writing in 1923, maintained that Texas Baptists showed little interest in foreign missions until fellow Baptists "were called by the Lord into foreign fields."[61] He noted that more than thirty missionaries had gone out, "among them some of the brightest and best Baptist sons and daughters."[62] One of them was his niece, Kate Carroll, daughter of B. H. Carroll.

The financial stewardship Texans demonstrated for the cause best illustrates the increased interest in missions. Texas Baptists had given $9,345.96 to foreign missions from 1845 until 1879. They gave $77,667.69 during the first decade of the Bagbys career; an 850 percent increase over the past thirty-four years. During the same decade, only three other states in the convention gave more to foreign missions than Texas had in the previous thirty-four years. Most states showed a dramatic decline. The fact that Texas experienced a drought during the decade makes the figures even more significant.[63] Texas Baptists not only supported the Bagbys, the Taylors, and others, but they also became a significant component of the Southern Baptist foreign mission enterprise. During this time, pledge amounts from Texas Baptists began to meet or exceed those given by the more established states in the South.[64]

Hawthorne wrote Anne that Tupper had asked him to appoint two prominent ministers in Texas to represent foreign missions in Brazil and Mexico. He chose B. H. Carroll to represent Brazil and A. T. Spalding of Galveston to represent Mexico.[65] B. H. Carroll preached the missionary sermon at the Southern Baptist Convention in 1882, emphasizing the work in Brazil, and a large collection was received. It is fitting, then, that the first funds the Bagbys received after settling in Brazil were from B. H. Carroll.[66] Carroll and others promised to raise support and "hold the rope" for the young missionary couple. They kept their word.

Texans like R. C. Burleson, R. C. Buckner, L. R. Scarborough, E. Y. Mullins, and George W. Truett continued the Texas tradition of supporting the Bagbys in Brazil, both financially and through evangelistic campaigns.[67] Other people like John Hill Luther, Roxy Grove, Fannie Breedlove Davis, and A. T. Hawthorne also contributed their talents and influence toward the missionary cause. Strong connections and friendships existed between the Bagbys and the most influential Texas Baptists of their day.

From the beginning Anne Bagby viewed herself as a vocational missionary called to Brazil—not just a missionary's wife. Her desire to master Portuguese and teach small groups of women and children served as a model to women in Texas.[68] Her familial relationship with Baylor College for Women continued and blossomed into an educational outlet for many missionary children from Brazil and future missionary women from Texas.

Baylor College for Women sent many women to Brazil as either teachers or missionaries:

> Annie Luther Bagby (1880), Kate Stevens Crawford Taylor (1881), S. E. Johnson (1892), Laura Barton Taylor (1895), Mrs. J. E. Hamilton (1899), Bertha Mills Pettigrew (1902), Sallie Milford Rouse (1904), Alyne Guyness Muirhead (1907), Mary Shannon Stapp (1909), Kate Carroll (1910), Grace Cisco Taylor (1915), Lola Cook Ingram (1918), Gertrude W. Morgan (1919), Mrs. Truett Davis Clifton (1920), Grace Bagby Cowsert (1920), Bertha Lee Hunt (1920), Alice Bagby Smith (1920), Callie Perrin Wilcox (1920), Nora E. Hawkins (1921), Bernice Neal (1921), Marjorie Taylor Stanton (1921), Caroline Smith Taylor (1921), Margaret Johnson Porter (1922), Jennie Lou Swearingen (1922), Blanche Ham Bice (1923), Waller Ray

Buster (1923), Ura Hallmark Crouch (1923), Essie May Fuller (1923), Ione Buster Stover (1923), and Ana Fitzgerald (1924).[69]

Other graduates supported the mission cause from home. Emma McIver Woody helped establish the Woman's Training School at Southern Seminary. Kitty Lackey Stokes aided Mina Everett in the establishment of the Woman's Training School at Southwestern Seminary. At one time, Baylor College for Women claimed a larger percentage of foreign missionaries than any college in the convention: more than forty women left the college to serve on the mission field.[70]

Baylor College for Men also produced several missionaries for the Brazilian cause. The Foreign Mission Volunteer Band was formed in December 1900 and elected William Bagby as one of its first honorary members. On June 7, 1902 H. H. Muirhead was elected to send letters to "missionaries around the world inquiring about special facets of missionary work in their countries."[71] Both Lottie Moon and Bagby responded, urging the student volunteers to consider their particular country.[72] Bagby and Taylor also spoke frequently to the band when they were on furlough. Minutes from the organization recorded Taylor speaking at their meeting on at least ten different occasions.[73]

Missionaries who came out of the Baylor Foreign Mission Volunteer Band at Baylor College for Men, and were assigned to Brazil, included F. M. Edwards, H. H. Muirhead, Taylor Bagby, J. J. Minchin, Willson Bagby, Lester Bell, L. L. Johnson, E. A. Ingram, Orlando Falcon, R. S. Jones, and F. A. R. Morgan.

Not all of the Southern Baptist missionaries in Brazil were from Texas, but a majority represented the state. Missionary conventions and conferences in Brazil, as a result, included the renewal of friendships forged during college days in Texas. This lent a cohesiveness to the Brazilian mission which those on other Southern Baptist foreign fields did not experience. In a spiritual sense, the Bagbys helped accomplish what the Confederate exiles longed for but never attained.

The Bagbys fostered this strong connection with Texas through their writings and preaching engagements while on furlough.[74] Missionaries on furlough in the United States were expected to make speaking tours, and "personal appearances by missionaries were highly prized in small-town America."[75] Newspaper advertisements announced the arrival of a foreign missionary and gave an open invitation to all churches in the area to come and hear the latest "missionary intelligence."[76] The Foreign Mission Board kept William Bagby as busy on furlough as he had been on the field.[77]

Bagby traveled throughout the southern United States during his furloughs, but spent most of his time in Texas. An incomplete list of the cities he visited explains his role as a lightning rod for foreign missions among the churches in Texas. Places at which he spoke about Brazil and foreign missions in Texas included: Waco, Temple, Belton, Austin, McKinney, Gainesville, Dallas, DeLeon, Hamilton, Comanche, Gatesville, McGregor, Greenville, Moody, Brownwood, Abilene, Mexia, Athens, Paris, Bonham, Ferris, Sherman, Fort Worth, Weatherford, Lone Oak, Buckner's Orphan Home, Savoy, Tyler, Oceola, Lampasas, Desdemonia, Bryan, Calvert, Corsicana, and Baylor University.[78] After his speeches, Bagby took up a collection for foreign missions and asked for pledge cards for monthly gifts toward their work. He also used these meetings to find prospective missionaries and to talk to them about Brazil. Missionaries like Mina Everett, Roxy Grove, and others not only helped the Bagbys in Brazil, but they were also proud publicity agents once they returned to the United States.[79]

William Bagby grew up admiring Texas frontier preachers, and his life work consisted of helping scores of transplanted Texan preachers in the Christianization of Brazil. As a young man, he saw the effects of economic disaster on a region, but he also noted the results men like B. H. Carroll, R. C. Buckner, R. C. Burleson, Colonel Speight, A. T. Hawthorne, and Major Penn could accomplish for the kingdom of God through perseverance. Bagby also would persevere in his new work because others promised to "hold the rope" for him at home; a promise they did not break.

The early Baptist missionaries developed Brazil like their contemporaries had developed the Lone Star State. In fact, there was a camaraderie between Texans and Brazilians because they faced similar issues of education, evangelism, and financial support. This *esprit de corps* would culminate in joint mission projects between Texas and Brazil in the twentieth century. William and Anne Bagby were both known as visionaries, but neither could have pictured the influence they would have on Southern Baptist foreign missions and Texas Southern Baptists when they began their work in Salvador, Bahia.

PERSECUTION AND THE
STATE OF ROMAN CATHOLICISM

Nothing mobilized the home front to pray and give to the mission cause like the missionary's personal accounts of persecution. Dramatic accounts began to pour out of Brazil and flood the pages of the *Foreign Mission Journal* of the Southern Baptist Convention. Bowen's prophetic words concerning "clearing the forest of fierce savages before the land could be planted" proved a concise commentary on the early work of Brazilian Baptists.

Attempting to avoid persecution, the missionaries held their meetings on the second floor of the mission building in Salvador, Bahia, but even then, bones and rocks were thrown at the windows. One evening, stones "the size of a man's fist and larger" were hurled at the house, and the Bagby children "narrowly escaped being struck."[80] On another occasion, a heckler turned off the gas at the street below and left the meeting hall pitch black without lights.[81] Some of those who attended the meetings were only there to cause trouble and began stamping and hissing in the middle of the service to disturb the assembly. The missionaries were often forced to ask for police protection on the nights they preached.[82]

Sometimes, however, not even the police could safeguard the missionaries, as the following account by Bagby demonstrates:

> One day I baptized a young man in the sea, in a lone place, hidden away. A mob of our enemies looked for us but could not find us until the baptism was over. They threatened to kill us that night if I preached in a certain place where I had promised to be. We went there and had a great crowd of people in the house of a poor family who had invited in the people to hear us. We began to sing, and soon a crowd of evil-minded persons gathered outside, and began to hoot and howl, and throw rocks and bones and hands full of wet sand in at the windows, and rocks on the tiled roofing. The only lamp

we had was smashed, a stone struck a girl on the head, and then I was struck and knocked senseless. I was picked up and carried into an inner room, and the blood was washed off.[83]

The police arrested Bagby shortly afterwards to "protect" him from the crowds. The missionaries concluded the arrest was mainly to save face before the people. Z. C. Taylor, who was not at the meeting, commented the next day to Will, "Bagby, that wound is the greatest thing I ever saw. I wish I had been there too. I'd rather have a wound like that on my head than to have the crown of any king in Europe."[84] Baptismal services and marriage ceremonies were the most frequent places the missionaries encountered persecution.[85]

Persecution had a significant impact on the formation of Brazilian Baptists—it solidified their preaching and purpose.[86] It did not surprise Bagby and Taylor to encounter persecution in their work. The same thing had happened in the dramatic accounts in the book of Acts. They believed, in fact, that persecution actually authenticated their ministry as consistent with the New Testament. They could point to the book of Acts and claim that persecution always followed the "true" preaching of God's word. They also contended that the behavior of the priests was like that of the heathen, thus dismissing the legitimacy of Catholicism. Persecution created a sense of passion and destiny in the missionaries and their Brazilian converts that would propel them numerically into the thousands during the Bagbys missionary service.[87]

Most of the persecution arose out of the simple fact that the Catholic church in Brazil had lost a great deal of power and prestige and faced immense difficulties in its ministry to Brazilians. The melding of church and state never allowed the Catholic church in Brazil to develop a distinct identity because it "was almost totally reliant on the state for its infrastructure and the processes for exercising influence."[88] Brazil experienced a tumultuous relationship between church and state in the nineteenth century with "outright conflicts, suppression of religious orders, expulsion of hierarchies, and restrictive legislation on education."[89] As a result, Brazil boasted a Catholic heritage, but one that had lost its spiritual legacy. E. H. Quillen wrote that, "Catholicism was in the imbecility of years."[90]

A shortage of priests, religious ignorance, an inadequate sacramental life, the inability of priests to minister to the rural population, insufficient organization of the laity, prevalence of superstitious practices, and propaganda methods of some Protestant groups from the United States were the most significant problems facing the Catholic church in Brazil.[91] The flood of immigration and resulting Protestant missionary invasion posed a threat to the Roman Catholic Church armada, and it could do little to defend herself. Persecution became its chief method of preservation.

The Baptist missionaries and their sharp critique of Catholicism through preaching and the printed word exasperated an already tenuous situation. Bagby, never shy in sharing his views on Catholicism, wrote:

> Those who have studied Italy, Spain, Portugal, Austria, and Mexico, at home, socially, morally, and religiously, can form some idea of the condition of this nation in those respects. It is the same sad lesson of religious slavery, moral canker, and corruption! But no form of words, no picture of pen, no relation of circumstances and isolated series of facts can fully convey a conception of the darkness and gloom which fills the moral sky of each and every papal land. The most puerile and debasing superstitions, the most delusive fictions, the most merciless soul-tyranny and mental bondage: the most corrupting dogmas, the most shameless perversions of truth and unblushing enforcement of error, everywhere prevail, while the mired-dignitaries of Rome calmly survey the field of normal night, and their agents debase, pervert, and oppress.[92]

Baptist attitudes toward Catholicism soon incited the Catholic priests to reciprocate. The priests believed the missionaries were merely "advance agents of an American policy to dominate them."[93]

Roman Catholicism accomplished four things in Brazil, according to William Bagby: it "trained a favored few, proclaimed an adulterated gospel, established with governmental aid some hospitals, and enslaved the nation to a commercialized religion."[94] He continued by listing four things that Catholicism failed to do for Brazil: "to give the Bible to the people, to bring peace to the troubled heart, to give Brazil a personal and visualized Christianity, and to develop their moral sense."[95] Bagby and Taylor set about to develop methods and strategies that would answer the failings of the Roman Catholic Church in Brazil.

The missionaries believed several religious practices in Brazil contributed to the moral bankruptcy of the nation. The Brazilian's lack of reverence for Christian holidays mortified the Baptist missionaries. William wrote his sister Ermine:

> Christmas day here was a warm bright day of merriment, folly, and idolatry! . . . The pagan rites and ceremonies of Rome were paraded in all these shrines and cathedrals, and the degradation and immorality of the myriad dupes of priestcraft were displayed! . . . My heart grows sick where Satan's power is supreme and deadly! Oh! for the day when the holiness and peace of the Gospel shall illumine this abyss of shame and misery![96]

Bagby also wrote, "The Lord's Day is made a season of revelry and sin, or of toil, or of idleness."[97] Most employed Sunday as a normal workday. Many spent the Sabbath "in dancing and recreations" while others "in drunkenness and brawls."[98] Very few, Bagby maintained, "think of spending the day in devotion or religious rest."[99]

The superstitious nature of Brazilian Catholicism also troubled the missionaries. Bagby wrote, "Romanism is only heathenism with Christian names for its gods."[100] Like heathens, he maintained, "Charms are worn by men, women, and children . . . crosses and horns are placed on fruit stands, or hung up by the doorway, to keep away witches and evil spirits."[101] Brazilian peasants lived in "an enchanted world of evil spirits, magical powers, and powerful saints."[102] Adding to the problem were priests who charged for their services and promoted superstitious ideas to pad their pocketbooks. "The priests," Bagby judged, "are grossly licentious . . . almost all of them are living in open concubinage."[103]

American newspapers actively published Bagby's disparaging comments about Catholicism in Brazil. His criticisms bolstered Baptists in the United States who were just beginning to deal with the flood and frustration of Catholic immigration in their own country.[104] Immigration brought 1,250,000 Catholics to America in the decade of the 1880s, culminating in a population of 8,909,000. Baptists during the same period grew from 2,500,000 to 3,700,000. By 1910 the Catholic population was 16,330,000 and new bishoprics and archbishoprics were organized to minister to the burgeoning population. Rumors abounded among Southern Baptists that the Catholic church in the United States was going to wrench America away from Protestantism and give her as a gift to the pope in Rome.[105]

Excerpts from one of William's sermons, preached in the United States while on furlough, demonstrate his ability to capitalize on these fears to promote the foreign mission cause further. Catholicism, he maintained,

> . . . argues with equal bearing with the social and political interest of our people, country, and age. . . . It is, in fact, the history of a religion, which in every age since the first few centuries . . . and in every country inhabited by civilized man, has confined itself not to things of a spiritual nature alone, but has struggled with unparalleled energy for temporal power and political supremacy among the nations. It has ever shown itself determinedly antagonistic to religious and civil liberty. . . . But when in watching the course of events in American history, and the true interest of her people, we find an organization laboring with all the mad zeal of fanaticism, all the forethought, and the concentrated determination of Satanic malignity, for the overturning of the rights of American people: When also we see the stupidity and blindness of Americans to the tricks, machinations, and attempts at Catholic supremacy here . . . while even now poisonous and pestilential vapors, fraught with the breath of demons, rises up to stifle and choke the life throbbings of liberty and the pale and sickly hues of the day foreshadow the ghostly dominions of Popery: we think it a duty, obligatory upon some one, to attempt the arousing of the American mind to the unparalleled efforts of that body, and for our own eternal interests. . . . Romanism has for hundreds of years held almost universal sway . . . in South America . . . blasting and blighting the loveliest and richest lands of the world. . . . Catholics are flooding the land with their sable and bitter waters. . . . It is a vast army of 6,000,000 combatants, each struggling with burning heart, and single purpose, for the same great end. Seven great divisions cover the land, each ruled by a leader more sagacious than the greatest military

chieftain. 56 Bishops, 4500 priests, 4887 churches, 1400 chapels, and 1200 parochial schools show the magnitude of this ancient organization. One fourth of the population of the United States, they claim, is already Catholic in sympathy, and the whole gravitating toward it. . . . And what is the attitude of Evangelical denominations toward this dark cloud of on-sweeping desolation? Why Protestants are gently warming to their bosoms these vipers which shall sting them, gently caressing these angel-clothed emissaries of Satan.[106]

William Bagby's anti-Catholic stance both encouraged prejudice at home and justified the Southern Baptist presence in Brazil. Unlike the rest of Europe, the Protestant Reformation had not touched Brazil in the sixteenth century. In the eyes of many Southern Baptists, William Buck Bagby stood as a modern-day "Martin Luther," preaching against the abuses and corruption of the Roman Catholic Church.

PROBLEMS IN THE MISSION

Persecution from the Roman Catholic Church was not the only difficulty the missionaries faced, however. Problems boiled amongst themselves, too. Anne and Kate were competitive women, and this soon led to hard feelings in the mission. Feelings were hurt when Taylor asked Bagby to judge which of the wives spoke better Portuguese. William postponed his decision for three months because Kate was further along with the language than Anne, although Anne had been in Brazil eleven months longer.[107] Anne believed the climate also made them both irritable, and her pregnancy did not help matters.[108] Heated battles over housekeeping and proper respect drove the women even more apart. Kate wrote in her diary, "Struggle after struggle I pass through to love my sister."[109]

Years after the Bagbys left for Rio de Janeiro, Kate would still write Anne, asking, "I do not think you would have so much reason now to complain of being misunderstood. Do forgive and forget any and all my errors and please do write oftener and more sisterly."[110]

Differences in strategy also created internal problems in the mission and a desire among the missionaries for separate mission fields. William wrote Hawthorne:

> Bro. Taylor and Mrs. T. have entirely different ideas from ours on many subjects and while we regard them highly as workers . . . we are compelled to differ from them in many respects. . . . I believe we can manage to work here together successfully, for some time, yet I believe, in the future . . . it will be better for us to work in different fields.[111]

Although the personality conflict between Anne and Kate was also a prime motivator for wanting separate mission fields, William Bagby mentioned the problems of "congeniality" only to Hawthorne and Dr. Luther.[112] He guaranteed Tupper, "My idea of Brother Taylor as a worker and man and Christian is the highest. There is nothing between us personally."[113]

Bagby requested that the board start a new mission in Rio de Janeiro.[114] Funding would not be a problem. Bagby pleaded, "If the Board is not able to establish the new mission by reason of lack of funds, then can not one of us return home and raise funds by personal effort. . . . If necessary let one of us come home and plead the matter before the Baptists of the South."[115]

The Foreign Mission Board was slow to adopt Bagby's proposal, sensing that internal problems in the mission might be prompting the change.[116] The response of the mission was to report the advances being made in the Baptist cause and plead for a reconsideration.[117]

In March 1884 the Bagbys moved into another house in the suburbs, leaving the Taylors stationed in the mission building. Bagby reassured Tupper, "Someday when I see you, Doctor, I will tell you about how popular brother Taylor is with the brethren and friends here. He is a noble worker, and so is sister Taylor."[118] The board reconsidered the matter and recommended on April 7, 1884 that another mission be established in Rio de Janeiro, Brazil, staffed by William and Anne Bagby.[119]

Chapter 5

An Evangelistic Ministry: Rio de Janeiro

We do not see any reason why a missionary should be any less de-
voted to his business than a merchant or clerk and yet it looks as if some
of the missionaries who have come out here have not scrupled to take
advantage of the first slight pretext to return and all the money which had
been spent on sending them and supporting them for a year or two has
been thrown away—and worse than thrown away . . . Anyone coming out
with a mere romantic idea in his head will soon get enough of it, for there
are plenty of discouragements which will soon make themselves met, the
more particularly as a newcomer is necessarily kept from doing much
work until he gets the language—a merely lukewarm Christian wife is a
terrible drag on any missionary and we especially beg you not to overlook
this point . . . It is with genuine sorrow that we give up Bro. Bagby, yet
we feel that present circumstances render it necessary, his state of health
requiring him to live too far away to give pastoral duties the attention
which they demand. . . .

— Brother Irvine to Willingham[1]

MISSION WORK BEFORE THE REPUBLIC

The Bagbys left Salvador, Bahia, on May 25, 1884, for Santa
Barbara, Sao Paulo. After ministering to the American colonists
for a month, they arrived in Rio de Janeiro on July 24, 1884,
and lodged at a hotel until a suitable house could be found. Z. C.

Taylor was placed in charge of the Bahia mission while Teixeira was sent to Maceio to begin a new work on May 17, 1885.[2]

The separation of the Southern Baptist mission into three fields at Bahia, Maceio, and Rio de Janeiro forsook the conventional wisdom of other evangelical missionaries on the field. Other denominations chose to concentrate their efforts chiefly in one area. A. R. Crabtree commented forty years later that, "The weak and widely separated Baptist churches in Bahia, Recife, Campos, Bello Horizonte and Sao Paulo, seemed to many a useless scattering of forces, but today these throbbing centers of evangelism have placed Baptists far in the front ranks of all Evangelical denominations."[3] Ultimately, Bagby's plan for establishing a vast web of churches in different locations allowed Southern Baptists to influence a significant area of Brazil. The transition from one mission into three proved difficult, however.

The Bahia mission suffered financially from repeated requests for food by members who had been fired from their jobs because they had joined the Baptist church. The mission was not able to meet the financial needs of everyone; some left the church as a result. Immorality plagued the congregation and Taylor excluded several members from the fellowship. Bible sales continued to improve, however, and several excluded members were eventually restored. Persecution was never far off, and a few years later a young man attempted unsuccessfully to throw a bomb into the crowded meeting hall. A riot broke out when they apprehended the man, and Taylor was forced to release him before the police arrived. Missionary spirits sagged when the offering box was stolen from the hall shortly afterward.[4]

The mission at Maceio, Teixeira's hometown, met with great success, but persecution also followed the Brazilian pastor. One night while preaching, villagers gathered and began to hurl stones at the house where the believers were meeting. No injuries occurred and soon Teixeira's entire family had become Baptists. However, after a promising start, Teixeira died of yellow fever three years later.[5]

The Bagbys first efforts in Rio de Janeiro occurred at the boarding house of Eliza Williams, a member of Spurgeon's Church in England. On August 24, 1884, they organized the First Baptist Church of Rio de Janeiro with four members: Wil-

liam and Anne Bagby, Eliza Williams, and Mary O'Rourke. Jo-
anna Snyder joined the group shortly afterward. Bagby baptized
a former Presbyterian missionary, C. I. Mesquita, on January 29,
1885, but it was not until November 15, 1885, that he baptized
the first Brazilian convert, Castorina Adelia Soares, who joined
the church. Meager results induced Tupper to recommend that
Bagby minister in the rural areas where response might be
greater. Ignoring Tupper's advice, Bagby continued to preach
mostly in English to his congregation in Rio de Janeiro.[6]

Wishing to reach Brazilians, the Bagbys rented a preaching
hall in the great square of the city, but they drew little attention.
So, Will and Anne took their folding organ out on the street and
began to play and sing. Brazilians stopped to listen to the music,
and the next night many came to the worship service.[7] Anne
Bagby had sung to Confederate and Union soldiers during the
Civil War in the United States and now used her talents to bring
the Americans and Brazilians together. The Bagbys soon found
that services composed of singing with short prayers and brief
Scripture readings had a tremendous impact on the spiritual interest of the Brazilian population.[8]

Two new ideas for reaching the Brazilians were initiated in
Rio but were never fully developed. First, Will and Anne considered opening an orphanage. Orphans filled the streets of the
larger cities of Brazil, and the Bagbys had compassion for them.
They hired two servant girls who had been disowned, or "or-
phaned," from their families and "adopted" two English girls
who had lost their parents. When they wrote home for financial
support, relatives and friends responded favorably, but the
board did not think it a good idea, so they discontinued the
plan. Second, after the Bagbys first furlough, Anne attempted to
start an industrial school to teach sewing, but the board rejected
this idea and she discarded it too.[9]

For the most part, Will implemented the methods for reaching Brazilians developed in Salvador, Bahia, in Rio de Janeiro.
Will continued to publish the *Baptist Catechism for Children,* Ford's
History of the Baptists, and an eight-page monthly newspaper. He
hired a Bible colporteur, and lay evangelists were encouraged to
preach in the homes of believers. The new church also employed
a woman to visit and read the Bible to Brazilians. A Sunday

School was organized, which increased worship service attendance.[10]

C. I. Mesquita, who had worked with the Presbyterian missionaries for fourteen years in Rio de Janeiro, was hired by the board as an assistant to Bagby.[11] The Bagbys considered him "an indispensable element in the frail little church, preaching, visiting, and writing untiringly."[12] He edited the newspaper Bagby published and "preached an average of thirty sermons a week, once fainting in the pulpit from sheer exhaustion."[13] Unfortunately, when the board reduced his salary in 1887, he accumulated a large debt, and his family began to starve. The result was his dismissal on March 27, 1888. Bitterly, Mesquita accused all missionaries of being "traitors of the Gospel."[14]

The Foreign Mission Board appointed several missionaries from Texas to the Brazilian mission in 1885: Mr. and Mrs. E. A. Puthuff, Mr. and Mrs. C. D. Daniel, and Miss Mina Everett. The board also appointed E. H. Soper, an Englishman, to aid the mission. All, however, were forced within a few years to return to the United States or England because of health problems.[15] Reinforcements, no matter the length of their sojourn, came at an expedient time. After an intense bout with yellow fever, Bagby himself was forced to return to the United States on furlough in March 1886.[16] He wrote the board, "I have been very near death's door, but the Lord has raised me up. I am very, very weak. My physician urges the necessity of a sea voyage and I have determined to return to the United States for a few month's visit with my family."[17] The board's financial problems would prevent his return to Brazil for fifteen months, and his speaking schedule while on furlough yielded little rest.

Reaching the United States, Bagby traveled extensively in Texas with A. T. Hawthorne to raise funds for foreign missions. He also made preaching tours through several states in the southern United States including Virginia, Missouri, Arkansas, and Mississippi. In fact, he visited thirty churches in Mississippi during the first two months of 1887. The physical toll was brutal. He wrote Anne that he was suffering from headaches, digestive problems, colds, fever, sore throats, and homesickness.[18]

During the Southern Baptist Convention of 1886, Bagby met with missionaries Taylor of Rome, Powell of Mexico, and

Diaz of Cuba. They discussed their common problems in ministering to Roman Catholic countries. They also decided that T. P. Crawford's new ideas of self-support on the mission field would not affect the Foreign Mission Board.[19] Anne chose to stay with her parents while on furlough and ignored several requests by Will to attend state conventions. He wrote Anne from the Missouri convention saying, "All regretted so much your absence. Many came especially to see you, and were extremely disappointed."[20] Will had to accept a quilt for Anne during the Arkansas convention, much to the consternation of the women present.[21] She did, however, speak to several ladies' groups at the Louisville convention with good results.[22]

Anne confessed openly to her father that she was not sure she wanted to go back to Brazil. She had enjoyed her visit at Baylor College for Women, which had recently moved to Belton, Texas. The loss of the Bagbys second child to scarlet fever during the furlough also made the return trip difficult. She exclaimed, "I ought to be the happiest of women, but the reaction of the visit home has tried me sorely. I am more of a baby about you than ever before."[23]

In spite of Will's fund-raising attempts, the Foreign Mission Board asserted that they could not send the Bagbys back to Brazil because of a lack of funds. B. H. Carroll feared that this would seriously harm the raising of funds for foreign mission work in Texas.[24] In response, A. T. Hawthorne formulated a plan to recruit twenty men who would contribute $2,000 above their regular mission giving for the Bagbys. Will's father was one of his first solicitations.[25] The plan worked and Bagby wrote Tupper in April 1887, "If the Board is not willing to let me go, advancing the money myself, then let me resign my place as missionary of the Board and I will try to support myself in Brazil as best as I can."[26] The Bagbys set sail for Brazil a month later, still missionaries of the Southern Baptist Convention.

The Bagbys brought Maggie Rice, a single woman missionary, to Rio de Janeiro on their return. Anne described her as:

> Truly a treasure to have in our home: so intelligent, energetic, and cheerful, and at the same time considerate, easily pleased, helpful and devoted to the work. She has fine health and is fast

gaining Portuguese and has begun to work among the people
as well as teach school in Portuguese.[27]

Rice's school soon numbered twelve little girls, ten of whom
were Brazilian, and one little boy. Will wrote his sister, "We could
not have found anyone, outside of our own families, who would
have pleased us in every thing as she has done and is doing."[28]

Unfortunately, after serving on the field for eighteen
months, Maggie Rice contracted yellow fever and passed away.
Anne shared, "Oh, it is heart-rending to remember her groans,
she did suffer so! She died at eight o'clock November 26—with
the coming of the dread black vomit." Anne continued, "I can't
tell you how my heart bleeds tonight. . . . Oh, how I do miss
Maggie! We were perfectly congenial and she did pet and humor
me so!"[29] Miss Rice's death frightened the Bagby children who
thought their mother might "go to heaven" also.

Emma Morton was strongly moved during a revival service
in Louisiana when she learned of Rice's death. One morning
during her devotions, she believed she had received a command
to go to Brazil in Rice's place. She contracted yellow fever on her
way to Brazil, but she recovered and began to teach in the Bagby
home a few weeks after her arrival.[30]

In 1889, after almost six years in Rio de Janeiro, and with
the departure of most of the missionary reinforcements, Bagby
was left with the overwhelming job of running the mission by
himself. He wrote his sister, "This leaves me alone, to conduct
the mission, act as treasurer, correspond with papers, teach Portuguese, visit the people, superintend Sunday School and preach
four times a week!"[31] Anne wrote Tupper, concerned about Will's
health. She reminded Tupper that she now had to cook to spare
the money usually spent on house cleaners.[32] The board considered closing the Rio mission, but decided against it when their
deliberations began to hurt the work.[33]

Brazil became a republic on November 14, 1889. This event
brought a political change that eventually would create an un-
equaled opportunity for Southern Baptists in that country. The
Bagbys, however, could hardly celebrate. In December 1889,
Will wrote the board:

I cannot live on the salary allowed me. I asked for the least amount on which we can live here and keep our health. . . . I write this therefore to ask the Board either to give me the salary asked for or guarantee me exchange at two and a half milreis to the dollar. . . . If this is impossible, then much to our deep sorrow, we will be compelled to return to the United States immediately. I have nearly nine years experience of the cost of living here and of the trying nature of the climate and I know just what is absolutely necessary to health and strength. . . . You mention the reduction in salaries of our Chinese brethren, but it costs more to live here. The Presbyterians pay their missionaries 3 times as much here than in China. . . . God knows that I do not want to lay up money. I only want support. This I have not had since I returned to Brazil. . . . I have supported my family only by selling a little property I had at home and by some help from my family. We live with the greatest economy we know how to practice and can see no way of living cheaper.[34]

Anne wrote her parents saying, "The work is so promising it would break our hearts to leave just now!"[35] She also wrote Tupper chiding, "I can not believe that the Board does not appreciate our situation in regard to exchange. Surely it has had experiences in this line in other countries before!"[36] In the future, Brazil would be Southern Baptists' most productive mission field, but at that moment, the Bagbys questioned the ability of the Foreign Mission Board to continue the cause.

THE REPUBLIC OF BRAZIL

When the Brazilian parliament established a republic in 1889, evangelicals had been in Brazil almost thirty years and the results had been meager. The Presbyterians were the most prosperous and had sixty-three churches, thirty-two ministers, 2,966 members, and thirteen schools. The Methodists had eight churches, seven ministers, 346 members, three native preachers, twenty preaching stations, and two schools. Southern Baptists had five churches, 241 members, twelve missionaries, and three native teachers. In a country of 10,000,000, the three main evangelical denominations had converted only 3,553 individuals. The missionaries attributed their lack of numbers to the denial of religious liberty in Brazil. The coming of the republic presented them with a proving ground for their hypothesis.[37]

The Brazilian revolution in 1889 was the culmination of several antecedent events and did not surprise political observers. The most significant event was the liberation of the slaves on May 13, 1888. Political pressure mounted after Princess Isabella, in the absence of the emperor, abolished slavery and offered no recompense to the slave owners. The political leadership of Dom Pedro II had become increasingly absent in Brazil during the years leading up to the founding of the republic. Not only were the great landowners offended by his answer to the slavery question, but the Catholic church and army found themselves increasingly alienated by the emperor's decisions. The general public, with the rise of industry and a middle class, also began to face social and political problems that the monarchy was either unable or unwilling to address.[38]

Having established the republic with a *coup d'etat* on November 14, 1889, the leaders of the new congress wished to pattern their government after the United States. Several weeks before the revolution, Aristides Lobo, future Secretary of the Interior, had visited Bagby and consulted with him on domestic policy questions concerning marriage and divorce.[39] During the discussion, Lobo also copied the United States Constitution by hand and questioned Bagby on various aspects of the separation of church and state.[40] The Brazilian Constitution ultimately resembled the United States Constitution in many ways including: freedom of speech, freedom of the press, trial by jury, religious tolerance, separation of church and state, and civil state marriages.[41]

The results of the new constitution were devastating to the Catholic church in Brazil. No longer supported by the state, the church was forced into open competition with Protestant groups who had been gaining a foothold for several decades. The Catholic church became more dependent on Rome and unwisely adopted European organizational structures that were irrelevant to the Latin American culture. Large numbers of foreign priests and nuns entered the country and the church started new seminaries, but those they attempted to reach perceived them as alien transplants. Protestantism, as a result, became an inviting alternative on Brazil's spiritual landscape.[42]

The conflict between Catholicism and Protestantism was

not based solely on religious grounds. Protestant missionaries pointed to the "civilization, progress, and advancement of Protestants and Protestant nations," whereas Catholic nations "dominated by priests were rated as third-class nations."[43] The consensus was that "business leaders and owners of capital . . . were overwhelmingly Protestant."[44] Because of recent technological advances, many Protestants believed they could evangelize the world in their generation. Indeed, for the average American, the spread of national influence and Christianity were "but different sides of the same coin."[45] There was an unapologetic synthesis, then, of commercial and religious endeavor. Protestants believed they could achieve what they saw happening in their industrial empire for God's kingdom: world conquest.[46]

Missionaries of the period assumed that the Anglo-Saxon race was superior to all others and under obligation by God to take salvation to the world.[47] One Southern Baptist missionary summed it up: "Southern Baptists believe that all that is best in the United States is the result of Christianity; and that the religion which is capable of uplifting this country and maintaining as high a level as we enjoy, is also capable of uplifting other nations and greatly improving their plane of living."[48] Southern Baptists like the Bagbys believed it was their duty to influence the institutions, ideologies, and cultures of less fortunate countries. When the occasion demanded it, "the big brother ought to help and direct the little brother—sometimes, perhaps, box the little fellow's ears!"[49]

It is not surprising, then, that there was a correlation between the rise of the United States as a world power and the heightened interest in foreign missions between 1890 and 1920. At the beginning of this period the United States sent out 934 missionaries to foreign lands, but by the end there were more than 9,000 missionaries.[50] Often, missionary increases followed political gains. In India, Korea, and Japan, improved diplomatic relations also enhanced the position of missionaries and resulted in greater success.[51] Brazil proved to be another example.

Observers noted that most Brazilian Protestants were in the newly created middle class, and their conversion to Protestantism was "a result and concomitant of social mobility."[52] Protestantism did not create a new middle class, but it took advantage of the emerging bourgeois in Brazil: "The new faith won most of its followers among the social classes whose formation and chances of social ascent were directly affected by structural changes imposed by the emerging industrial order."[53] People seeking to leave the lower class enrolled their children in Protestant mission schools. With their education, these children rose above their lower economic surroundings. Mission schools helped cause a "virile class which eventually became the backbone of a better community life."[54]

The missionaries and their supporters believed many things needed to be changed in Brazil:

> As soon as the masses in Brazil are delivered from the vices that infest the country they will rise morally and economically and socially, thus forming a middle class which will make the country strong against foes within and without. There are many enemies to the progress and welfare of Brazil. . . . Owing to lack of proper hygiene, many of the cities of Brazil have a very high death rate. . . . The immorality of the priesthood is one of the worst enemies to the welfare of Brazil . . . drinking and gambling are found everywhere in Brazil. All grocers sell wet goods, and in addition there are drinking shops all over the cities. Lotteries are run by both state and church in Brazil.[55]

Protestant missionaries pounced upon the disparity in moral values between themselves and the Catholic priests. Southern Baptists introduced a new set of morals—a new world view—in Brazilian culture.[56]

Without question, when Brazil became a republic, more than the political sphere changed. Solomon Ginsburg, a contemporary of the Bagbys, celebrated the fact that Brazilian Catholicism was losing the culture war as well. He believed Brazilians were adopting American ideals, American methods of business, and were ready for American democracy. Spiritually, people were becoming more receptive to the gospel.[57] His analysis was correct for the most part. In fact, the Bagbys always maintained that they would not have been as successful in Brazil had it not been for the freedom of religion resulting from the new republic.[58]

WOMEN AND MISSIONS

In the midst of the changing political and cultural landscape, the fledgling Baptist work began to tap an underutilized resource: the women of Brazil. Anne Bagby established the first Baptist Woman's Missionary Union in Brazil at First Baptist Church, Rio de Janeiro, in 1889. The new organization met a need for Brazilian women who formerly belonged to the "Sociede de Irmas de Maria," a Roman Catholic woman's group established to meet the needs of the poor.[59] An outgrowth of the women's work was ministry to children, and F. F. Soren organized the first children's society at First Baptist Church, Rio de Janeiro, in 1903.[60] With the creation of the Woman's Missionary Union (W.M.U.) in Rio de Janeiro, Anne influenced Brazilian women much like she had inspired Texas women ten years earlier.

The impetus for woman's missionary unions in the Southern Baptist Convention was the training and support of single women for work on the foreign field. As early as 1883, Southern Seminary in Louisville allowed women to attend classes, but they did not grant them diplomas for their studies. Toward the beginning of the twentieth century, however, a strong grassroots movement formed, seeking diploma programs for women going to the mission field. In 1895 the Texas delegation to the national W.M.U. meeting proposed a training school in Texas under the leadership of Mina Everett, a returned missionary from Brazil. The delegation prepared a paper to be read at the convention, but Annie Armstrong blocked their presentation from the agenda. Armstrong's actions injured her relationship with Anne Bagby.[61]

Annie Armstrong's inflexible approach toward the training of single missionary women only encouraged the movement, and Texas Baptists finally established a training school for women in Dallas, Texas, on October 3, 1904. Early teachers included J. B. Gambrell, Mary T. Gambrell, George W. Truett, and George W. McDaniel. Six students from Buckner's Orphan Home enrolled immediately, and the school eventually merged with Southwestern Baptist Theological Seminary. The training school degree required two years of study in subjects such as kindergarten education, expression, theology, and music. L. R. Scarborough taught classes on personal work and evangelism. The training school also adopted Anne Bagby's proposal for a scholarship to be given to the woman making the highest grade in a Bible study competition.[62]

The movement among Baptist women in Texas was a miniature mural of Christian women throughout the United States. The Woman's Missionary Movement was incredibly large and played a significant role in the success of the modern missionary movement. By 1915 more than three million women filled the membership rolls of forty denominational female missionary societies. Foreign missions captured the hearts and imaginations of women like no crusade had in America. The Woman's Missionary Movement was larger than the Student Volunteer Movement, the Laymen's Missionary Movement, or any other women's movement of the nineteenth century.[63]

Women, during the period between the Civil War and World War I, could take a "role in a worldwide enterprise that claimed ultimate significance yet was entirely consistent with their ideology of home and motherhood and their theology of sacrificial service."[64] The main focus of every woman missionary supporter was to reach out to her sisters in foreign lands and give them the gospel.[65] In America, "the limitations placed on women in other societies and programs for their liberation and education were spoken of continually, especially by women missionaries and women mission leaders."[66]

American women supported those who went to the mission field both financially and emotionally. In truth, before women rallied behind the mission cause, potential missionaries had no sustaining base of support in America.[67] But because of the mission movement, women began to exercise greater economy at home, sacrificing their money for their sisters in foreign lands. Missionary publications also encouraged Protestant women to provide emotional support. As a result, women in the United States did their best to make sure that every missionary felt "that they were never far from the thoughts and prayers of a supportive sisterhood in America."[68]

Women missionaries on the field like Anne Bagby cherished emotional support from those at home. Difficulties facing missionary wives included raising children, teaching a variety of subjects, and opening the missionary home as a frequent stopping place for visitors. Another problem was mastering the language, and the resulting sense of hopelessness and discouragement that often accompanied their studies. The most difficult task of all for a married woman was ". . . to bid farewell to her husband, who might be away for three months at a time, and to bear stoically all the fictitious reports of his illness, accidents, or death which inevitably filtered back to here as a form of psychological persecution on the part of the Roman Catholics."[69]

Women on the mission field also wrote home, encouraging and exhorting their female supporters concerning the Protestant errand to the world. Ermine Bagby, Will and Anne's oldest daughter, wrote an epistle that reveals some assumptions of her clan. Ermine believed that many American women did not live up to their pious responsibility. She wrote, "Oh, how can our American womanhood disregard the desperate situation in the world, and plunge itself in recklessness and selfish pleasure?"[70]

After graduating from Baylor College for Women, Ermine noted American women on the ship during her return trip to Brazil "disregarding all ideas of modesty in dress, especially in their costume parties, smoking, and even gambling."[71] She exclaimed, "The whole world, America included, cries out for the ministrations of a God-fearing, sane, wholesome womanhood."[72] Ermine reminded her American readers of their "wonderful spiritual heritage," claiming that the "keen minds and physical beauty" of American women made them "well-nigh invincible," but they were "denying their birthright of piety and religion."[73] Too many women, Ermine believed, were "shirking the great duty and privilege of motherhood and filling their days with useless, cheap fripperies which they fondly believe are real activities."[74]

MISSION WORK AFTER THE REPUBLIC

After Brazil declared itself a republic, Southern Baptist mission work began to grow exponentially. New missionaries reinforced the Bagbys in Rio de Janeiro, along with native helpers. William Bagby developed a network of churches that could be reached by rail and maintained from the mission station at Rio de Janeiro. He began churches in Juiz de Flores, Santo Aleixo, Campos, Para, Bello Horizonte, Niteroi, and Parahyba.[75] Preaching stations, the first step in formalizing a church, were organized in several other cities, and the Rio mission also continued to minister to the American church at Santa Barbara.

The work in the city of Campos illustrates how quickly Baptist work could explode in an area. Bagby visited Campos in 1891, rented a meeting hall, and ordered seats for worship services. After Will preached and seven were converted, a native helper, Senhor Amaro, moved his family to Campos and began a full-time ministry. A few months later, fourteen presented themselves for baptism, some of whom had walked sixteen miles to the meeting. In fact, Amaro and Bagby baptized fifty converts in the first seventeen months of the church's existence. Solomon Ginsburg was put in charge of the Campos church in 1894. Later that year, Bagby requested an exchange of fields, but the board denied his petition. At the new church building dedication on April 21, 1898, Bagby estimated a crowd of approximately 1,000 attending. Campos became the most fruitful Southern Baptist mission in all of Brazil.[76]

Wealthy immigrant businessmen often used their influence to help start Baptist churches. A prime example was the work in the city of Santo Aleixo. Mr. Arthrington, the owner of a large cloth factory in Santo Aleixo, invited Bagby and Soper to launch a Baptist church. Santo Aleixo was six hours from Rio de Janeiro, three hours by sea and an additional three hours by carriage. Situated in a remote area, no priest visited the town on a regular basis. Bagby conducted five services in a crowded house and, in spite of torrential rains, more than forty indicated a desire for salvation. They put a native helper, Senhor Menegez, in charge of the work.[77]

The work in the city of Juiz de Flores demonstrates the powerful effect a native helper could have on a mission church. In 1889 C. D. Daniel initiated work in Juiz de Flores, Minas Geraes, and asked Bagby to help him with a revival service soon afterward. Several Brazilians were converted, and the missionaries quickly organized a small church. Although the people of Juiz de Flores showed great interest and Bagby baptized three believers on his second trip, after a year only three members remained. Consequently, Bagby rented a small hall for preaching and left a native helper, Domingos de Oliveira, as pastor in his absence. Four members were added quickly because of Oliveira's work. When the city priest began to publish articles against the struggling church, two open air meetings were broken up when hecklers threw stones at the meeting hall. Nevertheless, the work of Oliveira prospered, and soon the church was large enough to have a missionary.[78]

The role of native helpers in the achievements of the Rio de Janeiro mission was decisive. Native helpers allowed the ministry to expand at a greater rate than would have been possible otherwise. William Buck Bagby also converted and trained significant leaders for the future convention from among the native helpers. Three native helpers who played a strategic role in the Brazilian mission were Tomaz da Costa, F. F. Soren, and Theodore Teixeira. Ginsburg, a contemporary of the Bagbys, contended that if Bagby had only converted and trained these three men, his ministry in Brazil would have been considered a success.[79]

Tomaz da Costa accepted Christ in a worship service held by William Bagby in 1889. As a layman, he preached effectively in the states of Para, Bahia, and Sao Paulo. For many years he served as corresponding secretary of the Brazilian Baptist Foreign Mission Board.[80]

Thomas da Costa invited his friend F. F. Soren to a service in 1890. Bagby's preaching deeply moved Soren. Looking for answers, Soren borrowed a Bible from his priest and began reading in Genesis. The commandment against graven images shattered his faith in Catholicism, and he arranged for an appointment with Bagby to discuss salvation. After lunch on a Sunday afternoon, Soren received Christ in an upstairs room of the Bagby home.

After a few years in the Rio church, Soren responded to a call to the ministry and forsook his business career, moving into the home of missionary J. J. Taylor on January 10, 1893. He remained there for ten months studying the New Testament and other religious subjects. Missionary J. L. Downing then arranged for him to go to William Jewell College in Liberty, Missouri. Bagby eagerly anticipated Soren's return to Rio de Janeiro after graduation four years later, but he was bitterly disappointed when Soren decided to continue his education at Southern Seminary in Louisville, Kentucky. Bagby wrote, "Soren will never in his life perhaps be as much needed in Brazil as right now."[81] He added, "Frankly, for my part, if he does not come out now in our time of great need, I care little if he ever comes or not."[82]

The Foreign Mission Board wanted Soren to become pastor of the First Baptist Church of Rio de Janeiro, a position recently vacated because of the sudden death of missionary McCarthey from yellow fever.[83] Soren's initial reason for not returning to Brazil was based on his unwillingness to work with missionary Ginsburg. However, when Ginsburg did not take over the Rio mission as planned, and Soren continued his studies in the United States, most of the missionaries and the leadership of the church at Rio de Janeiro believed him to be a lost cause.[84] Soren left the seminary and returned to Brazil on October 3, 1900 after an absence of a little more than seven years.[85]

The evaluation of Soren's abilities by the church at Rio and the missionaries on the field proved to be incorrect. Soren served as president of the first Brazilian Baptist Convention, as the first president of the Baptist Education Society of Brazil, and as pastor of the First Baptist Church, Rio de Janeiro, for forty years.[86] He also served as trustee of the Rio Seminary and College as well as the Girls' School of Sao Paulo. A fund-raising trip to the United States by Soren in 1915 allowed First Baptist Church, Rio de Janeiro, to build a new 1,000-seat auditorium.[87]

Theodore Teixeira was converted in 1891 by William Bagby. F. F. Soren taught him English, and Teixeira ultimately translated several English works into Portuguese, including Broadus' *Commentary on Matthew*. As assistant editor of *O Jornal Batista*, and later editor-in-chief, he made a lasting contribution to the progress, unity, and development of Brazilian Baptists.[88]

DIFFICULTIES ON THE FIELD

Although William Bagby wrote that "no impediment" stood in the way of the missionaries after the revolution in 1889, moral lapses by native workers, financial distress, and health concerns plagued the ministry for the next ten years.[89]

Moral problems among native helpers were a significant problem the Bagbys faced during their ministry in Rio de Janeiro. Their experience with Dr. Ottoni was a good example. Ottoni was converted and baptized by Z. C. Taylor in Bahia, but he later moved to Rio de Janeiro. The ex-priest gave up a sizable government pension after his conversion, and he impressed all the missionaries with his oratorical abilities. Having mastered five languages, his writing and editing skills held great promise for the Baptist cause.[90]

Ottoni married a woman from the Baptist church at Juiz de Flores and began his ministry at First Baptist, Rio de Janeiro, in 1895. The church guaranteed half his support and ordained him on the dedication Sunday for the new church building.[91] Moral and financial problems began to appear in June 1896. Apparently, when the Foreign Mission Board cut Ottoni's appropriation from $600 a year to $200 at the beginning of 1896, he found it hard to make ends meet.[92] He borrowed money secretly from anyone who would lend it and then lied when he could not repay his debts. Members of the First Baptist Church, Rio de Janeiro, lost all confidence in Ottoni and refused to let him preach.[93] The church later tried to restore him against Bagby's objections, but Z. C. Taylor ultimately employed him as a secular instructor in the school at Bahia.[94]

Ottoni's case study also illustrates the second major problem the Bagbys faced ministering in Rio de Janeiro—financial distress. The Foreign Mission Board found itself in financial difficulty the last decade of the nineteenth century due to Gospel Missionism, or Crawfordism. At the 1888 Southern Baptist Convention in Richmond, T. P. Crawford contended that American missionaries to China could only reach the Chinese by dressing and eating like them. He "insisted that native Christianity be self-controlling and self-supporting from the beginning."[95] Crawford claimed that the Foreign Mission Board was wasting missionary funds on the mission field and not the best way to get funds to the missionaries. Remarks like "If you give $10 to Foreign Missions, it takes $9 of it to get the other $1 to the missionary" became the slogans of Crawfordism.[96] The principal result of Crawfordism in Texas was the withholding of funds by Baptist churches, a fact which drove the Foreign Mission Board further into debt.[97] During this time of financial difficulty, the Bagbys initiated a plan to give 10 percent of their income back to the board to relieve its deficits.[98]

Wildly fluctuating exchange rates in Brazil also contributed to the financial distress of the Bagbys and made the monetary foundation of the mission enterprise shaky. William Bagby wrote early in 1890 that he had barely been able to survive on the field for three years because of harsh economic times. Although the Bagbys received private contributions from home, they still found the economics of Brazil hard to weather.[99] Bagby and missionary J. J. Taylor wrote the board in 1900 with the sad news that debt was a certainty for both the mission and themselves because of poor exchange rates.[100]

Tension over a lack of giving on the home front and fluctuating exchange rates on the field caused the board to accuse the Bagbys of misappropriating mission funds in 1896. Bagby denied the charge and responded that since trust was a crucial element in the board's relationship with its missionaries on the field, the board should allow the missionaries to make decisions which benefitted the work.[101]

Health concerns, however, were the greatest obstacle the Bagbys faced during their ministry in Rio de Janeiro. Anne Bagby suffered repeatedly with morning sickness during several pregnancies and experienced a miscarriage.[102] The heat in Rio adversely affected Will's health and forced a furlough in 1892.[103] Upon his return, he developed a plan to exchange fields with missionary J. J. Taylor in Sao Paulo. The board approved the plan, but the missionaries later rejected it themselves.[104] Lack of personnel kept Bagby at the Rio mission longer than the board desired. They implemented a plan for Bagby to live in the city of Nova Friburgo, moderate in climate, and commute to the Rio mission. The strategy succeeded until the work could no longer flourish with Bagby that far away. After yet another threat of resignation, the board granted him a furlough in 1900.[105]

In spite of several obstacles, William and Anne Luther Bagby achieved notable success in Rio de Janeiro after Brazil became a republic in 1889. Bagby organized a Property Holding

Association in 1894 to safeguard the legal rights of property owned by Baptists. The need for such an association arose after the Rio church purchased its first building that year. The dedication of the First Baptist Church sanctuary at Rio de Janeiro in 1894 marked the culmination of five years of consistent pleas to the Foreign Mission Board by William Buck Bagby. Soon after the dedication of the new building, Bagby organized the six churches of the Rio mission into the first Brazilian Baptist Association, "The Union of Churches of Christ in South Brazil."[106] Self-support and evangelistic cooperation were the main topics discussed at the introductory meeting, and "As an immediate result of the meeting, the churches began to raise funds for the support of a traveling missionary."[107] Although the meetings were sometimes spirited, Bagby maintained the "missionary ground" and was pleased at the progress of the native Brazilians. Following the example of First Baptist Church, Rio de Janeiro, all of the churches in the association began to send a quarterly offering to the Southern Baptist Foreign Mission Board in Richmond for foreign missions.[108]

Five years after the formation of the republic, and subsequent freedom of religion, the Bagbys work in Rio de Janeiro had grown from a faithful few to an association of six churches. During their tenure in Rio de Janeiro, the Bagbys trained and assisted native helpers. They also persevered through financial and physical problems. The Bagbys continued to spread the gospel of the Bible explicitly, and American democracy implicitly, into the Brazilian culture.

Chapter 6

An Educational Ministry: Sao Paulo City, Sao Paulo

The sky was blue, the ocean warm, the children joyful. Dressed in their white uniforms, all the children of the Sao Paulo school had joined with members of First Baptist Church, Sao Paulo, to celebrate the ninetieth anniversary of Brazil's independence. Men and women talked casually as children made sand castles and challenged the waves on Jose Menino Beach. "This is family," Anne cheered herself.

Every once in a while a game of hide-and-seek would come but then just as quickly it would go. Others hiked, some strolled the beach collecting shells and starfish. Anne watched as Willson and three friends pushed a row boat into the ocean. "My son is such a leader" she whispered to herself and smiled at him in approval.

Anne gazed at the children as they ate their picnic lunches and thought "it has been worth the hardships." Maybe they had struggled financially for years, maybe the Board had not supported like they would have wished, but seeing the difference her school was making in the lives of these hungry learners eased the pain. Eased the regrets. At least her own children had received an education that would not shame them when they returned to the States for college. They would be at the top of their class, she had made certain of that.

A shout went up from the boat and everyone turned and smiled. Youthful exuberance. Willson and his friends were playing a game. They were two hundred feet away from the shore waving their arms, shouting. The boys and their boat appeared and disappeared, the scene broken by the white billows. As Willson dove off the capsized boat, Pedro and Gillespie cheered him on. After a few moments the game was over. There was only the boat and Pedro and Gillespie.

77

Instantly, the crowd became silent. This was not a game, this was death! The sight of her son drowning clubbed Anne in the heart and punched the breath out of her lungs. She felt completely helpless as she paced the seashore. The ocean depths had swallowed up the life of her precious boy. The waves pounded at her feet as a persistent reminder. Willson was gone.

Two sailors were dispatched to the boat and rescued Pedro and Gillespie, unconscious from the ordeal. Will walked the coastline, searching for the broken body of his son. A nearby hotel owner relayed the sad news that he had never seen a corpse come to the shore in less than three days and then in an unrecognizable form. He had lived there for thirty years. Anne prayed, "Lord, if you have taken our boy's soul for yourself, allow us to have his body intact." Anne and Will sat down quietly and watched the shoreline. Three days was a long time to wait. But they would be there when Willson came home.

Everyone had dispersed when the bodies of Willson and Luiz Herbst washed up on the beach two hours later, lifeless but unharmed. "It is a miracle," Dona Ana, the hotel owner declared, "nothing short of a miracle."

EDUCATION IN BRAZIL

Historically, Brazilian educational efforts had met with dismal results. For the most part, the Brazilian government left education to the Catholic church. Those who acquired their training in Portugal were considered educated, while the rest of the population was regarded as unlearned. The result was an illiteracy rate estimated at 80 percent in 1872.[1] National concern over illiteracy escalated in September 1882 when a report given to the National Senate showed how far Brazil trailed behind the western world educationally. In 1890 the provisional government issued a decree making primary education free, gratuitous, and secular. Education became a responsibility of the states. This broke "the hold of the Roman Catholic clergy on the public educational system of Brazil and encouraged the older Protestant missions to enlarge their educational facilities."[2]

Education in Brazil was based on the Jesuit model introduced by early Catholic missionaries. The public school curriculum included spelling, reading, writing, and arithmetic. Private Roman Catholic schools added religious recitations. Professionally-trained instructors were the exception, and the schools allowed anyone with a high school or college diploma to teach. The students learned by rote and recited their lessons aloud. Thus, the brightest students might do one or two arithmetic problems a day if they did not need assistance. Discipline was severe, and teachers often paraded students who did not do their homework in the streets with donkey masks on their faces.[3]

New educational ideas from America began to influence Brazil in the 1870s, primarily through Protestant missionaries, who transformed the student-teacher relationship by encouraging classroom discussion. Their schools offered science classes that undermined rote learning and promoted intellectual curiosity among the Brazilian students. Protestants also established schools for girls, which became very popular with the upper classes in Brazil. Brazilians were eager to attend Protestant schools and master English so that American and English companies would hire them.[4]

From the beginning, Southern Baptist missionaries in Brazil saw the importance of education. First, E. H. Quillen recommended the formation of literary schools in 1879. Quillen's main emphasis was on academics, not the Bible. He did not believe that he should offer Bible classes during the day, but only at night, for those who showed an interest.[5] The Bagbys, however, believed schools could be a strong evangelistic tool. Bagby proclaimed, "Send your missionaries, establish your mission schools and the irresistible power of the gospel will go abroad in South America, and the land of the Southern Cross will brighten up with the resplendency of the Kingdom of Christ."[6] Will and Anne noticed the great interest Brazilians showed in the education of their children and recognized it as a possible means of attracting them to the gospel.[7]

Another reason Baptists were motivated to form their own schools was discrimination by unscrupulous Catholic priests. Although the constitution of 1890 declared religious discrimination illegal, many priests continued to persecute Protestant groups openly, especially evangelical children who attended Catholic schools. Sometimes, through pressure from the local Roman Catholic priest, missionary children were forced to bow before icons and accompany their classmates in Catholic processionals. The priests compelled Baptist students to attend mass. The children also received lower grades if they did not pray to Mary and were punished if they did not attend catechism.[8]

Finally, Baptist missionaries found illiteracy to be the chief opponent to their progress in Brazil and pursued the educating of their members as a result. A personal understanding of the Bible was basic to all Baptist beliefs, unlike the Catholic church, which relied on group participation and the primacy of the priest. Consequently, once a Brazilian accepted Christ and became a member of a Baptist church, education played a vital role in the development of faith. Baptist leaders offered classes for older Brazilian men and women so they could "stumble through the Gospel of John to pick out for themselves their own passages for memory work."[9] A 1950 study of illiteracy proved the impact of their efforts: Baptist congregations only had a 3.4 percent illiteracy rate.[10]

THE GIRLS' SCHOOL OF SAO PAULO

It was not until almost two decades after the Bagbys arrival in Brazil that Southern Baptist missionaries in Brazil began to focus more of their energy on education. In 1898 Misses Stenger and Wilcox, two single missionaries from Philadelphia, began a school in Bello Horizonte, Minas Geraes, with their personal funds. That same year Mrs. Z. C. Taylor started a school in Bahia. A wealthy coffee grower gave her $5,000 toward the enterprise, and the church at Bahia raised an additional $2,000.[11] In 1901 William and Anne Bagby purchased a school from Mrs. McIntyre in Sao Paulo City. Anne Bagby named the institution the Girls' School of Sao Paulo.[12]

The Girls' School of Sao Paulo originated in Campinas, Sao Paulo, under the leadership of Mrs. McIntyre, a daughter of the woman who housed the Bagbys at Santa Barbara when they first reached Brazil in 1881. Mrs. McIntyre moved the school to Sao Paulo in 1895. The school, named the *Colegio Progresso Brasileiro,* was a standard high school, the equivalent of an eleven-grade school in the United States. Supporters called it "Baylor College

John Hill Luther,
Anne Bagby's father

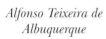

Alfonso Teixeira de
Albuquerque

Z. C. Taylor

Kate Crawford Taylor

First Mission meeting, 1892. Left to right (sitting): E. H. Soper, W. B. Bagby, Mrs. J. J. Taylor; (second row): Mrs. E. H. Soper, Mrs. J. L. Downing, J. L. Downing, Mrs. W. B. Bagby, Miss Emma Morton (second Mrs. Ginsburg), J. J. Taylor; (third row): Mr. and Mrs. W. E. Entzminger; (fourth row): Mr. and Mrs. S. L. Ginsburg.

Mary Ellis

William Buck and Anne Luther Bagby at time of sailing for Brazil

Anne L. Bagby, 1887

Oliver Halbert Bagby
Type—Brunette
Height—Five and one-half feet
Age—Twenty-six and one-half years

Anne L. Bagby

William B. Bagby

Dr. Bagby standing at site of first baptism

Bagby school 1907; Top grade and teachers

Classmates in the Bagby school about 1910

Student body of Sao Paulo Baptist School

Photo of early congregations

Lapa Church, Sao Paulo and Russian congregation—last church organized by the Bagbys

Gym class Bagby school, 1911

*First Baptist Church, Rio de Janeiro, 50th Anniversary Celebration, 1934.
Thomas da Castoa (first lower left), Theodoro Teiheira (seventh from left, first
row), Dr Bratcher (extreme right, first row), Mrs. Soren (third lower left),
Founders (center), deacons, and wives.*

of the Southern Cross" in honor of Anne Bagby. By 1925, fourteen different nationalities attended, five languages were taught,
and the school had 400 boarders. Three of Anne Bagby's daughters—Ermine, Alice, and Helen—helped with the school.[13]

Several factors prompted William and Anne Bagby to purchase the institution and focus on educational work in Sao
Paulo. First, after living in Rio de Janeiro for seventeen years,
they found the standard of living in Sao Paulo to be higher, and
they spent their yearly appropriation too quickly. They hoped
income from the school would prevent the embarrassment of
asking the board for more funds. Second, the Bagbys believed
their children were not receiving an adequate education in Brazil. These fears abated when Ermine excelled at Baylor College
for Women in Belton, Texas, but the educational needs of her
remaining children persuaded Anne to purchase the school.[14]

Will, however, revealed his main motivation for building
Baptist schools to Dr. Willingham, corresponding secretary of
the Foreign Mission Board:

> The conviction has grown upon us after these years of experi-
> ence of the work in South America in all its phases, that it is of
> the utmost importance that the building up of some denomi-
> national educational institutions follow and accompany the
> work of evangelization. The stability and growth of our work
> absolutely demand this. . . . We must educate in self defense.
> Our Baptist boys and girls must be educated by us, or we are
> going to lose many of them. Romanists, Infidels, and Pedo-
> Baptists are building up their schools and if we Baptists have
> not our own, our young people will either grow up in igno-
> rance or else drift off from us.[15]

The Bagbys had recently lost a friend to the Presbyterian church.
They knew the young man for twenty years, but the influence of
the Presbyterian school convinced the boy to change denominations. Anne Bagby shared with Willingham:

> We even helped support him at the Presbyterian school and
> when, a few months ago, he joined the Presbyterian church . . .
> it cut us to the quick. Both Presbyterians and Methodists have
> gained many a girl and boy of Baptist parentage, just because
> we have no school of our own in the South.[16]

The Bagbys believed they could reach the "better classes" through education work and teach the children of fellow missionaries. The purchase price of $2,500 included furniture, a building, and patronage. The school was already paying all running expenses through its tuition. The Bagbys began the school with a promise of financial help from Annie Armstrong and the Southern Baptist W.M.U., but the funds never came. Anne Bagby wrote her father asking him to petition privately former students for the funds to purchase the school. She implored, "Please do not ask anyone to help who does not love the Cause."[17]

The Foreign Mission Board refused to help with the school financially because it had not approved the purchase in the first place. Offering an alternative plan of funding in 1901, Anne wrote the board, asking that their rent allowance of $600 be granted a year in advance. The Bagby family intended to live in the school building because of its large size. The board approved the request. In 1902 they wrote the board again and asked for rent two years in advance or the school would have to be sold. Anne was concerned that their furniture would have to be auctioned off, and that the mission's credibility would be ruined if the money was not forthcoming. The Sao Paulo mission entreated the Foreign Mission Board for help promising, "all future receipts from the school, above current expenses, after the debt is paid, will go directly to the work of our mission."[18] The board was concerned that the school would cause the Bagbys debilitating stress, but Will responded that the weight of the debt was their only dilemma. Again, the board approved their request.

The Bagbys asked the board to appoint Ermine as a missionary to Sao Paulo when she returned from Baylor College for Women in 1903. The board appointed Ermine and she taught daily in the school. Because of the dire financial times, Ermine planned to be a self-supporting missionary and only drew a salary to help pay off the school debt. In March 1904 William Bagby wrote: "Our school is doing finely. We have sixty scholars, and four teachers, besides my wife and myself. I myself do little teaching . . . am devoting my time to evangelistic mission work chiefly in Santos, Jundiahy, Villa Americana, Limeira and Campos."[19] He also requested an advance for rent for 1905.[20]

They finally paid the school off in March 1905, but three

months later Anne Bagby wrote that they must either have more financial help from home or sell the school. The Bagbys planned to approach the Methodist Conference to ask them to buy the school, already two months behind on expenses. Anne Bagby wrote, "Were it not for the blaspheme of it, I would be tempted to say that Jesus did not suffer all that we suffer here, that he did not know the debt string."[21]

Educational work had its own set of problems. Teachers were scarce, and the different missions vied for newcomers and dissatisfied workers already on the field. Alyne Goolsby wanted to go to Sao Paulo to help the Bagbys, but Z. C. Taylor pressured her into staying at Bahia.[22] Annie Thomas, a native Brazilian, was appointed to do school work at Sao Paulo but chose to do missionary work instead. Anne Bagby wrote the board fuming over the loss of yet another teacher, wishing some guidelines would be set concerning appointees.[23]

Will agitated the board when he brought Miss Ross from the United States, presuming her support as a kindergarten teacher. He wrote back that private talks with Dr. Porter and G. W. McDaniel, leading members of the board, had convinced him the board would support a good Baptist kindergarten teacher in Brazil.[24] The Bagbys consistently felt cheated in their school appropriation. The board responded that their school was twice the size of other Baptist schools and should not need as much assistance as a result. Will responded, "So we are . . . but in order to get these pupils we have to pay at least twice as much for teachers as the others do!"[25]

Early in 1910 the Bagbys wrote the Foreign Mission Board wishing to turn over control of the school. They requested that a board of trustees be elected representing all the missions in southern Brazil. They did not want the Sao Paulo mission to have sole control because of friction between the school and the mission. The board agreed. Bagby wrote again confessing that the school was $1,613 in debt, but he offered a plan to have the institution out of debt in two years. Anne Bagby wrote Willingham: "Can't you understand, that we do not want the school except for the good it is doing and when will you cease to listen to the jealous prattle of our enemies? If this school is a money-making establishment, why don't they begin one?"[26] The board responded that they would give no additional financial help to the school.[27]

Colegio Progresso Brasileiro continued to grow and the board assumed total ownership of the school in 1918. The board purchased a piece of property covering a full city block on a hill overlooking the city. The Judson Centennial Fund and the Seventy-five Million Campaign made funds for the effort possible.[28]

Anne influenced Southern Baptists in Brazil and the United States through her work at the *Colegio Progresso Brasileiro* in several ways. First, the fact that her school was twice the size of any other Baptist school made it the flagship school for Southern Baptists in Brazil. Until 1939 the school was also the only one specifically for young girls. The school made a significant impact on other Baptist schools in Brazil through its annual kindergarten teacher training program. Anne designed the program to prepare and place kindergarten teachers in Baptist schools in Brazil. Will wrote in 1917, "From our girls we have furnished four teachers for the college in Rio de Janeiro, two for Campos, one for Bahia, one for Santos, one for Parana, and three for the school itself."[29]

Second, Anne influenced Brazilian and United States Baptists through the Anne Luther Bagby Student Aid Fund established at Baylor College for Women, Belton, Texas. Elli Moore Townsend wrote, "Evangelism is crippled for lack of Christian teachers and ministers to carry out the work. So the evangelistic and educational forces must join hands in this great task."[30] They organized the Anne Luther Bagby Student Aid Fund to help children in Brazil who needed monetary assistance to attend school. Scholarship programs like the one named after Anne Bagby were often the only means for promising lower-class children an escape from the grinding poverty in Brazil.[31]

Finally, Anne saw education as the best prospect for reaching the upper classes in Brazil. She considered the Girls' School of Sao Paulo to be her chief contribution to the Baptist cause in Brazil, and she claimed that "schools had an important function in establishing new denominations."[32] The Girls' School of Sao Paulo was unashamedly Baptist. Classes opened and closed singing a hymn or reciting the Lord's prayer.[33] Anne proclaimed:

The exquisite engraving "A Little Child Shall Lead Them" hangs on our wall and we take its title as our school motto. . . . What better Agent is there for disarming prejudice than to send to their homes daily these small Gospel advocates of clean lips, ready hands and feet, sunshine faces, and patriotic hearts, who love the Savior of the world, love their country and their flag? If the Sunday School is universally acknowledged as an evangelizer, what can be said of the school that uses the graded International Sunday School lesson in every room five days in the week, which is the case in this school?[34]

She asked Willingham, however, "Is it right to teach these children to love Jesus when their parents do not know the result of such a belief?"[35]

Whatever the motives of the missionaries, many public officials and significant Brazilian national leaders benefitted from a Baptist education, including:

Gilberto Freyre (Sociologist), Julio Goncalves (Assistant to the Ministerio do Interior), Maria Amelia Daltro Santos (Educator, Professor at Instituto de Educacao of Rio), Necco Pinto (Head of the Health Department of the state of Pernambuco), Jose Munguba Sobrinho (Professor of Latin in the Colegio Americano Batista), Manuel Avelino de Souza (Pastor First Church of Niteroi, President of the Brazilian Baptist Convention, Professor of Homiletics in the Seminario Teologico do Sul do Brazil), Djalma Cunha (Seminary President), Helcias Camara (Home Board Missionary), Arnaldo Porto Poggi Figeuredo (President of the Colegio Americano Batista, Recife), Camara Dubois (Poet), Alberto Stanger (Director of the Ginasio Batista de Vitoria), Almir Goncalves (Pastor First Church of Vitoria).[36]

Second-generation Brazilian Protestants occupied important positions in all spheres of Brazilian life.[37] They excelled because of the educational legacy of Anne Bagby.

DENOMINATIONAL LIFE

William and Anne Bagby not only influenced Brazilians through their educational enterprise, but they also contributed to Brazilian denominational life during their ministry in Sao Paulo City, Sao Paulo. Will initiated the first Brazilian National Convention in 1907, serving as the first corresponding secretary of the Brazilian Foreign Mission Board, and organized the Baptist Publishing House of Brazil. Anne was at least partially responsible for the decision by the Foreign Mission Board to divide Brazil into two missions, north and south.

The need for a national convention among Brazilian Baptists was inevitable due to the organization of the mission. First, they formed churches, followed by associations. The need for some type of "national association" followed spontaneously, and Bagby laid the groundwork for such a meeting in 1906. The missionaries decided to meet on June 22, 1907, the twenty-fifth anniversary of the organization of the first Baptist church in Brazil. They agreed the site should be Salvador, Bahia, the first mission site of Southern Baptists in Brazil.[38]

The impetus for the Brazilian Baptist Convention may have arisen out of the celebration of the silver anniversary of Baptist work in Brazil, but a spiritual awakening that swept across Brazil beginning in 1905 also fueled the need for a convention. The awakening caused numerical growth in the churches, a deepening of spiritual life among believers, and increased religious activity. In the first quarter of 1905, 600 were added to the churches by confession of faith, 750 more joined in the second quarter, and there were nearly 3,000 additions by the end of the year. Evangelicals in Brazil increased their membership by 13.5 percent in 1905 alone. Results of the awakening among Southern Baptists in Brazil continued for several years. At the first meeting of the Brazilian Baptist Convention in 1907, Baptists reported almost 5,000 members; by 1910 they reported 9,939; by 1920 the total was 20,135; and by 1930 almost 37,000 members. The establishment of the convention met the critical need for more organization among Baptist churches, as suggested by William Bagby.[39]

Missionaries Bagby, Deter, and Ginsburg organized and publicized the convention; all of the male missionaries in Brazil met in Salvador, Bahia, on June 22, 1907. Forty-three representatives from thirty-nine churches convened to organize the Brazilian Baptist Convention. William Bagby preached the quarter-century sermon.[40] He wrote his impressions of the meeting to Willingham:

> Soren gave us a noble sermon on Sunday morning which set the key for the Convention. It was a fervent and soulful plea for national evangelization, and stirred all our hearts with new impulse and mighty ambition. . . . Oh that God may mightily stir our brethren in the United States to send us the men and women we so sorely need! We most heartily united in building up in Rio Janeiro a central College and Seminary, and in strengthening our schools in Sao Paulo, Bahia, and Pernambuco, as well as establishing new schools in other mission centers.[41]

F. F. Soren was chosen as president to put the "Brazilian brethren in the front."[42] Brazilian leaders continued to be elected president in future conventions for the same reason. The constitution and bylaws were modeled after those of the Southern Baptist Convention in the United States. The Brazilian convention also adopted the New Hampshire Confession of Faith.[43]

Although the convention exercised little centralizing influence over its various boards in the coming years, and was not a legal entity until the adoption of a new constitution in 1955, the organization of a national convention marked the beginning of a period of expansion by Southern Baptists in Brazil. It set in motion the development of home and foreign missions, the production of literature, the establishment of institutions for Christian and theological education, and the general promotion of the work.[44]

The convention elected William Bagby, F. F. Soren, and A. L. Dunstan to serve on the Brazilian Foreign Mission Board. In the first meeting of the board, Bagby was elected corresponding secretary.[45] He presented the following resolution to the newly formed convention:

> The Gospel which we preach is essentially missionary. "Go" is the first word of the Great Commission. "Go" is the first order given to every believer in Jesus. The history of Christian missions is the history of Christianity itself. We believe that the time has arrived for Baptist believers in Brazil to begin a movement to help in the preaching of the Gospel beyond the

national frontiers. We have unevangelized countries here in
South America. In a few of these, there are some two or three
preachers where people are in deep darkness and ignorance of
the Gospel. Among these are Bolivia, Peru, Ecuador, Colom-
bia, Venezuela and Chile. . . . While we have not a Baptist Mission in Chile there are about 900 Baptist believers. A letter recently received by the chairman of your committee states that
some of the missionaries of the Missionary Alliance and about
900 of their members are really Baptists and want to be organized into Baptist churches. It would seem that the time has
come, brethren, for us to send to Chile one of our brother missionaries of Brazil to help in the organization of Baptist
churches.[46]

The convention elected unanimously William Buck Bagby as
their representative to Chile.[47]

Bagby traveled to Chile, arriving in Santiago on April 3,
1908, after a twenty-two-hour train ride over the Pampa moun-
tains of Argentina. Bagby organized the work with a Baptist missionary from Scotland named McDonald, and returned to Brazil
on May 15, 1908.[48] The Brazilian Foreign Mission Board paid
the expenses of his trip. Brazilian Baptists were unable to continue the work, however, and turned it over to the Southern
Baptist Foreign Mission Board. While Bagby was in Chile, Z. C.
Taylor made plans to visit Portugal.[49] Solomon Ginsburg visited
Portugal later as a representative of the Brazilian Baptist Foreign
Mission Board.[50]

At the turn of the twentieth century, Southern Baptists in
Brazil recognized the need for a more organized publishing
mechanism. At the 1900 missionary meeting, the missionaries
decided to publish one denominational paper, *O Jornal Batista*.
They organized a society called the Baptist Editing House, and
Bagby reported on the society to those in the United States:

> Thousands of tracts have been issued from its press. *The
> Journal Baptists*, a Baptist weekly, is published and has a grow-
> ing circulation. The Society is also issuing an eight-page paper
> for Sunday School workers. It has also published a book on
> baptism, entitled *Fiat Lux*, and a translation of Dr. Torrey's
> famous little book, *How to Bring Men to Christ*.[51]

At the missionary meeting of 1902, all agreed that the publication of supporting literature continued to be critical. They adopted a plan to strengthen the publishing house in Rio de Janeiro. All the missionaries agreed to try to raise several thousand dollars for its use in the coming year, and they made an appeal to the Foreign Mission Board for $3,000.[52] Because the Baptist Editing House was not set up according to Brazilian law, however, the missionaries were forced to reorganize into the Baptist Publication Society in 1905.[53]

Will was elected first president of the Baptist Publication Society in 1905. Missionaries Deter and Dunstan served on the executive committee of the society along with Dr. Miranda Pinto, a Brazilian. Missionaries Bagby, Crosland, Reno, and Z. C. Taylor served on the advisory board. Deter was elected as director of the publishing house and editor of *O Jornal Batista,* replacing missionary Entzminger who had contracted leprosy. The board asked Z. C. Taylor to move to Rio and oversee the work of the publication house for a short time.[54]

During the Bagbys tenure in Brazil, Anne wrote few letters to the Foreign Mission Board. The ones she did write, however, gave an accurate glimpse into the struggles and accomplishments of missionary service. The Foreign Mission Board eventually carried out several of her ideas concerning the organization of the work. Such was the case with her proposal to organize the Brazil mission into two stations, north and south. She wrote Willingham in 1898 saying, "I think Brazil and Brazilian missionaries should be included in two missions, north and south, with their respective treasurers."[55] Positive changes included no appointment of a missionary without the consent of other missionaries, better regulation of house rent, and the inability to "steal" a worker from another field by offering a larger salary.[56] Ten years later, the Committee on South American Missions concurred:

> We recommend that our work in Brazil be reorganized and formed into two missions to be known as the North and the South Brazilian Missions. . . . The Board wishes to appoint a Treasurer for each of these two missions and requests that the brethren in their preliminary meeting suggest a man for each of these positions.[57]

During the 1910 meeting of the Brazilian Baptist Convention in Sao Paulo, and at the suggestion of the Foreign Mission Board's corresponding secretary, the organization committee proposed an agreement to divide Baptist mission work in Brazil into two regions. Each region would have an organized structure for fellowship, planning, and administration on the field. All of the missionaries joyfully agreed and the motion passed.[58] Although ten years had passed between her suggestion and reality, Anne celebrated her victory.

THE COLLEGE AND SEMINARY AT RIO

A lack of continuity and financial support characterized ministerial training on the Brazilian mission field until the first Brazilian convention. William Buck Bagby wrote in 1902, "How deeply I regret that the Board has declined to give us any appropriations for our young ministerial students for the coming year!"[59] In 1904 he wrote, "The continuance of our Theology class and its efficiency is a vital necessity to the welfare of our work in all this great State. We must depend on the young men whom the Lord raises up here and we must train them for future service."[60] Baptist missionaries recognized the need for ministerial training, but established no definitive plan until 1907.

While ministering in Rio de Janeiro, Will began to advance the necessity of training young preachers, and he organized classes under burdensome conditions. While in Sao Paulo, he promoted "Bible Institutes" at the Sao Paulo church, where he taught classes annually on subjects related to Christian service. Bagby wrote Willingham:

> I sincerely believe that the time has come when we Baptists cannot afford to neglect educational work. Evangelistic work should always occupy the first place, but educational work has certainly a most important part to play in our missionary enterprise, and we are losing, and are going to lose more and more, if we do not establish missionary schools on our various fields![61]

In 1904, the Foreign Mission Board of the Southern Baptist Convention decided that a national Brazilian college and seminary were necessary for the progress of the work. They wrote Bagby inquiring whether the best location for the schools would be Salvador or Rio de Janeiro. Bagby responded:

> It is utterly impossible for us to have one (and only one) training school for our whole Brazilian field! It would be like sending young men from Canada to Cuba. . . . There are three insurmountable difficulties in the way. . . . 1. That of race. In the whole of North Brazil a large part of the population is colored or mestizo. In South Brazil it is nearly all white. A mulatto preacher would not succeed down here! . . . 2. Climate. North Brazil is all hot and tropical. South Brazil is temperate and cool. . . . 3. Distance and expense. It would be impossible to send young men from one part of the country to the other. . . . At least two training schools are an absolute necessity.[62]

When the board wrote back that only one school was feasible financially, Bagby listed the reasons why Rio de Janeiro was the best possible site:

1. It is the national capital . . . and center of national life.
2. It is more accessible than any other city.
3. Its climate is favorable to health.
4. Its population is a mixed one, composed of Brazilians from the North . . . and South.
5. Owing to the vast improvement and rebuilding of a great part of Rio . . . the health of the city will be practically guaranteed.
6. Its libraries, museums, parks, national gatherings and legislative bodies may be made powerful facts in the training of young people.
7. Rio offers a field for Christian work for students unrivaled in all Brazil.[63]

Due to the influence of William Bagby, Rio de Janeiro was chosen as the site of the future college and seminary in Brazil.

The organizational meeting of the Brazilian national convention elected a board of trustees and commissioned this board to open a college and seminary at Rio de Janeiro in January 1908. They appointed missionary John W. Shepard to direct the new educational venture. Shepard came to Brazil as a direct result of hearing missionary Ginsburg speak in chapel at Southern Seminary while on furlough.[64]

The South Brazil Mission established the college and seminary in February 1908 under the direction of Shepard. They
held worship in the chapel every morning and special evangelistic services once each week. Bagby was appointed for a three-
year term as trustee of the Rio de Janeiro college and seminary.[65]
Shepard began to promote the importance of Christian education throughout the young denomination.[66] He presented a
focused vision of ministerial training:

> The principal need is trained Brazilian preachers for the num-
> berless undeveloped fields. . . . The institution should, there-
> fore, be a thoroughly equipped and endowed seminary. This
> should be the crown of all our educational endeavor and the
> more prominent feature of the composite institution located in
> Rio de Janeiro. . . . But we cannot hope to have a great semi-
> nary without the college training which will constitute the
> foundation for the theological course. This college can be
> made to meet the broader needs of the people for higher edu-
> cation and thus be almost, if not entirely, self-supporting in
> due time. The development of the collegiate department of
> the institution would be the natural outcome of the system of
> academies which will send their students to Rio for more ad-
> vanced study.[67]

By 1925 one-third of the money sent to Brazil by the Foreign
Mission Board was for the maintenance of schools. Half the
money sent to Rio de Janeiro was utilized at the Baptist College
and Seminary.[68] Missionaries of each state, especially in the
south, worked for the establishment of Baptist state schools in
their respective fields as rapidly as they could get funds from the
Richmond board.[69] Education had become the main thrust of
Southern Baptist mission work in Brazil.

In 1918 the Foreign Mission Board required six months of
language study at the Rio college for all new missionaries.[70]
Shepard continued to guide the college and seminary until his
resignation in 1931. The Rio de Janeiro institution matured into
the John W. Shepard College, South Brazil Baptist Theological
Seminary, and W.M.U. Training School.[71]

THE UNEASY ALLIANCE BETWEEN
EDUCATION AND EVANGELISM

William and Anne Bagby's marriage personified the wedding of evangelistic fervor and educational passion. Through their influence, this powerful combination of evangelism and education would become the chief characteristic of Brazilian missions. They did not initiate a new strategy, however. Baptists in America had emphasized evangelism and education on the frontier from the beginning. Southern Baptists believed schools to be an "aid to evangelization and a means of enlarging the Christian experience of the students."[72] They had to educate native workers if the work was to continue its upward spiral.[73]

The increased emphasis on education brought a new set of problems to the mission field. First, Catholics in Brazil and the United States accused the missionaries of offering education as a bribe to Brazilians to proselytize them.[74] Second, the missionaries felt uneasy when those at home learned that they employed Catholic teachers in Baptist schools because of governmental regulations. Sometimes even atheists and agnostics were hired due to a shortage of Baptist teachers, a fact which deeply disturbed those on and off the mission field.[75] William Bagby reported that the college and seminary at Rio de Janeiro were "composed of many non-professors of evangelical religion—of infidels, Catholics and Pedo-baptists who are our bitter enemies."[76]

Problems also developed between Shepard and the Rio College and Seminary board of trustees. According to the board of trustees, Shepard "attempted to exercise dictatorial and absolute control over the College and Seminary—using the Trustees as mere figureheads."[77] Board meetings were sporadic, and the trustees were "kept in profound ignorance as to the real state of the finances of the Institution."[78] They accused Shepard of transferring money from one fund to another without their approval and asked for his resignation.[79] The Foreign Mission Board denied their request.

In spite of these difficulties, Baptists in Brazil recognized the strong interdependence between education and evangelism in mission work. L. R. Scarborough commented on the correlation after an evangelistic tour of Brazil, "Evangelism needs edu-

cation if it is evangelized; education needs evangelism if it is ed-
ucationalized. Education must have a mighty heart-pulse of enthusiasm. Only the right sort of evangelism can furnish it. Evangelism needs the stabilizing, culturizing power of trained leadership."[80]

As more missionaries joined the Bagbys in Brazil, an uneasy
relationship between evangelism and education developed,
largely due to budget expenditures. From its inception, the Baptist witness in Brazil had been strongly evangelistic. Now, however, educational work consumed a substantial amount of mission money, a fact which made the more evangelistic missionaries uncomfortable. Will was very concerned about the strong bias
of education over evangelism in the South Brazil Mission. He
wrote the corresponding secretary,

> For some time I have wished that it were possible for me to see
> you, and have a long good talk with you and go before the
> Board, about a number of matters . . . principally about our
> educational institutions. . . . Some grave errors have been
> made and are being made. . . . Radical changes ought to be in-
> troduced and at once. We are neglecting evangelization, and
> putting the best new men, all, or nearly all, into the schools.
> The emphasis is being put on education to the woeful neglect
> of evangelization![81]

Further difficulties arose with the rise of Brazilian leadership after the formation of a national convention. In 1921 a conflict arose in the North Brazil Mission over the administration of
the school at Pernambuco. This conflict also affected the work in
the South Brazil Mission, but Bagby's relationship with Soren,
Teixeira, and Costa reduced the controversy.[82] One native
Brazilian leader wrote:

> We were slow to recognize the fact, but finally it became
> manifest that certain missionaries acted on the principle that
> financial assistance carried with it ecclesiastical domination.
> Their own words translated would be about this: Those who
> pay more govern more.
> We need financial help and cooperation from the mis-
> sionaries, but if these things are to be obtained at the expense

of independence and Baptist sovereignty, so far as we are concerned they cannot be accepted.[83]

The national leaders asked for autonomy in Brazilian churches, associations, and the national convention.

The Brazilian leaders wanted to administer the denomination with the cooperation of the Southern Baptist missionaries. Yet they also wanted expanded participation in the decisions and actual administration of the denomination. It was apparent to the Brazilian leaders that the missionaries did not trust their leadership. They maintained: "This in itself is a proof of the failure of the missionary work. If the missionaries were not able to develop national leadership in a mission field, their job was not well done. Instead of bringing to the mission field the liberating spirit of the Gospel, they fostered dependence and violated their very mission."[84] The missionaries found it hard to relinquish control of the denomination because of their prejudice. Membership of most Brazilian Baptist churches was divided equally between Caucasians and mulattoes. A Southern Baptist missionary noted that in many Brazilian churches there was "a sort of white aristocracy composed of people financially more prosperous than the darker-skinned."[85] He added quickly that this group did not "govern the Church by any means, but most of the officers were chosen from among the white members."[86] In truth, mulattoes were only allowed to govern in the absence of white leadership.

G. S. Dobbins, a professor at Southern Seminary, proclaimed the views of southerners on racial intermarriage:

The thought of intermarriage and consequent Negroid progeny is utterly repugnant to any right-thinking white man. One has only to go to certain Latin-American countries where this has occurred to be convinced of the terrible disaster which is involved. The standards of both races are lowered, the purity of the racial stock is destroyed and irreparable harm done to both peoples. No catastrophe to the human race could be quite comparable to the loss of racial integrity on the part of the American white people. So terrible is the contemplation of this contingency that it drives the average white man into an unreasoning rage if he dwells upon it as even a remote possibility. . . . The mulatto is less than a white man—and less than a Negro. . . . The greatest shame and obloquy the black race in America has suffered is not the fact of their slavery, but that their women have been debauched by white men, resulting in a host of mulattos who often combine the worst traits of both races.[87]

The problem centered on a prevalent theory at the beginning of the twentieth century that "racial mixture posed a threat to both blacks and whites alike."[88] From the beginning, the missionaries worked "with people whom they probably considered biologically damaged by racial intermarriage."[89] They believed, "no matter how much training the Brazilians received, they would never be able to attain to the level of ability of any racially pure person, especially those with predominant mulatto features."[90] Unfortunately, the race problem would linger after Will and Anne retired from the Brazilian field.

The Bagbys emphasis on education and denominational life during their ministry in Sao Paulo influenced the future of Brazilian Baptists. They initiated The Girls' School of Sao Paulo, the college and seminary at Rio de Janeiro, the first national convention, and the first attempts at Brazilian foreign missions. In the midst of educational pursuits, however, the Bagbys always insisted on the preeminence of evangelism in mission work.

Chapter 7

A Family Ministry:
Rio Grande do Sul

First, I mention in passing that ten days ago I passed my seventy-seventh milepost and am in the fifty-second year in Brazil! Oh, how glorious as never before, are the constant new openings and thrilling calls of new opportunities all about us! But what are we going to do about this, and are Southern Baptists going to abandon us, and are they no longer going to heed the calls of God's Spirit to come down and win this wonderland for Christ? How our hearts burn within us, as we read the sad news from our homeland in the Southern States, and the disheartening state of the Board's finances. Another cut is coming at the beginning of the new year, and it looks like it will be a mournful new year for us all. What we are going to do we cannot tell. My wife and I see no way or prospect of ever again visiting the United States, for we are practically now alone where we are, and we would be afraid ever to go to the homeland,—for the Board would likely not be able to send us back, and would likely tell us that we would have to stay there! The call now seems to be for all missionaries to stay there if they ever go, and it's dangerous to ever go to the United States again! I cannot even hope to go to the national convention in January for an entire lack of means . . . But we're far from giving up. In the far interior of the State we had a most exceptional experience. Nineteen persons, men and women, young women, girls and boys, boldly and gladly came out on the Lord's side. They stood up and declared themselves followers of Jesus, and we believe they are genuinely converted . . . .

— Bagby to Ray[1]

MISSIONARY CHILDREN

Anne Luther Bagby instilled a contagious enthusiasm for foreign missions in her children, much like she had inspired her husband in 1880. The Southern Baptist Foreign Mission Board appointed five of her nine children to service in Brazil. Of the remaining four, two died as toddlers, one drowned in a boating accident, and the last disappeared mysteriously one year before graduation from medical school in Galveston, Texas.

While it was true that one of Anne Bagby's main contributions to Baptists in Brazil was the legacy of her children, Brazilian culture facilitated her bequest. Nepotism was rife in Brazilian governmental service, and relatives of elected officials expected them to secure positions in the government for family members.[2] It is not surprising, then, that 14 percent of the Southern Baptist foreign mission force in Brazil by 1935 were the children of missionaries.[3] Most often, parents expected their children to pursue the missionary calling. One of the Bagbys' sons, Oliver, apparently found this expectation too demanding and vanished to avoid missionary service in Brazil.

ERMINE BAGBY SOWELL

The life of the Bagbys' first daughter, Ermine, spanned their ministry in "The Land of the Southern Cross." Ermine Bagby was born on July 27, 1881, at Campinas, Sao Paulo. Anne Bagby's sister, Zollie, wanted to raise Ermine in the United States, but the Bagbys decided to keep her on the mission field. Ermine forgot her Portuguese when the Bagbys went on their first furlough, but regained fluency quickly upon their return.[4]

Anne prepared Ermine for college by enrolling her in a Rio de Janeiro school that included classes in Portuguese, Latin, and French. Anne was still afraid, however, that her daughter would not do well in college in the United States. Her fears were unfounded. In 1903 Ermine graduated from Baylor College for Women near the top of her class. Will and Anne asked the board to appoint her to the Sao Paulo school when she returned to Brazil. The board approved the request, and Ermine worked in the Sao Paulo school to relieve the school's debt.[5]

The Foreign Mission Board sent Sydney Sowell, newly appointed missionary to Argentina, to stay with the Bagbys for a few weeks in November 1903. Officially, the reason for the trip was to acclimate Sowell to the South American culture. Secretly, however, the board hoped that a Bagby girl would fall in love with the young bachelor. Ermine's sister recounted what transpired next:

> Mother sounded a warning, "Now girls, I don't want that young man to run off with any of my teachers." What then was her surprise one day when, walking out on the front porch (where courting was positively forbidden), she found the blushing Mr. Sowell proposing to her own daughter! "It didn't take but a few minutes," he pleaded. But Ermine's answer was a longer process; he hopefully journeyed on to his destination and returned after two and a half years to claim his bride.[6]

Bagby wrote, "We all think that the Board made a wise choice of a man to open the great Argentina field!"[7] Ermine served with her husband in Argentina for thirty-three years. She taught in the Baptist Theological Seminary in Buenos Aires, helped to establish the training school in Buenos Aires, and organized a Bible Institute in Rosario. She died on August 18, 1939, from the same virus that had killed William Bagby two weeks earlier.[8]

LUTHER HENRY BAGBY

Luther Henry Bagby was born on July 10, 1883, at Salvador, Bahia. He died of scarlet fever on August 3, 1886, while the family was staying with Anne's father on furlough at Baylor College in Belton, Texas. Anne wrote in her diary:

> Just one month since our darling died and the heart still yearns for him and the bleeding wound flows, afresh at each mention of his name. I must lay this grief down afresh each day at the foot of the Cross. Only in this way can I meekly bear it and make it a refiner of my faith instead of letting it nourish a pitiful disposition.[9]

Will was on a missionary crusade and was not present at his son's death.[10] The loss of Luther made it difficult for Anne to return to Brazil. His death brought haunting nightmares, and Anne frequently placed flowers in a vase below his picture hung in their parlor in Rio de Janeiro.[11]

TAYLOR CRAWFORD BAGBY

Taylor Crawford Bagby, named after Z. C. Taylor and Kate Crawford, was born in Rio de Janeiro on September 29, 1885. He professed conversion at the age of six and was baptized five years later at First Baptist Church, Rio de Janeiro, by his grandfather, J. H. Luther. After their 1900 furlough, the Bagbys left him at the age of fifteen at Baylor University, but he returned to Brazil eighteen months later because of poor health.[12]

Taylor, nicknamed T. C., preached his first sermon in Santos, Sao Paulo, and decided to become a missionary to that city. He took some literary courses at MacKenzie College in Sao Paulo and occasionally filled the pulpit for his father in preparation. Will asked the board to give T. C. the appropriation of a native worker while he forged plans to return to Baylor University in Texas.[13] They granted the request.

T. C. returned to Baylor in 1905 and received his bachelor's degree in 1907. He served as pastor at Rayville, Louisiana, for eighteen months after graduation and then enrolled at Southern Seminary. After graduation from the seminary in 1912, he pastored at Kilmarnock, Virginia, for two years and married Frances Adams on January 1, 1913. Seeking to fulfill the missionary call heard years before, the young couple wrote the Foreign Mission Board seeking appointment to Santos, Sao Paulo. The board's response was "no."[14]

Willingham wrote Anne Bagby a brief explanation of why they did not appoint T. C.:

> I do not like to argue with a mother about her son, especially when I think he is as good a boy as your son Taylor, but we had our doubts about appointing him on account of marked peculiarities which we thought would hinder him in the work. It may be that in the course of time in this country, he will get

over these eccentricities . . . In fact, it is a source of great regret to some of us that he is so peculiar, and I hope that with a good wife, he will be able to remedy a number of his shortcomings along this line.[15]

The board was concerned that T. C. slept with his windows open at night, ate only two meals a day, and was not a "good mixer" in social settings. Anne Bagby was furious.[16]

Stung by the board's unwillingness to appoint T. C., the Bagbys suggested that their son return to Brazil and take control of the Sao Paulo school during their furlough. The board granted the Bagbys a furlough at the end of 1913, but the board did not assign T. C. in their place.[17]

T. C. and his wife moved to Santos, Sao Paulo, on November 28, 1914, and became self-supporting missionaries for several years. T. C. taught at a private school to pay their expenses, and the work flourished. The board reconsidered him for missionary appointment in 1917, but when they cut the number of applicants from eighteen to twelve, T. C.'s name was again eliminated. Will wrote the board saying that T. C. was very discouraged and would probably return to the United States as a result.[18] Finally, on June 6, 1918, the Foreign Mission Board appointed T. C. and Francine Bagby as missionaries to Brazil. T. C. and his wife continued their work in Santos and served for thirty-six years as Southern Baptist missionaries.[19]

WILLSON JAUDON BAGBY

Willson Jaudon Bagby was born in Rio de Janeiro on February 6, 1888. He helped in the Sao Paulo ministry as an organist, Sunday School superintendent, and leader of cottage prayer meetings.[20]

Willson left for the United States in 1907 to attend Baylor University as a ministerial student. After two years of study, however, Willson decided that he did not want to go into the ministry and returned to Brazil to enter the business world. The Foreign Mission Board declined to give William Bagby enough money for Willson's trip home, so the Bagbys sold an old piano for his passage of $200.[21]

The Girls' School of Sao Paulo and First Baptist Church, Sao Paulo, celebrated the ninetieth anniversary of Brazil's independence with a joint picnic on 7 September 1912. Tragically, Willson drowned at the celebration while attempting to save a friend, Luiz Herbst, in a boating accident.[22] Both Willson and Luiz were lost in the tragedy.

JOHN ZOLLI BAGBY

John Zolli Bagby was born on 10 June 1890 in Rio de Janeiro and died of meningitis on 6 August 1891.[23] Anne recorded his death in her diary:

> Our Babe is almost folded to Jesus' Breast—The Everlasting Arms are drawing him heavenward. He is lying in a stupor and I can't look at him any longer. I can be of no more use to him. He needs me no longer . . . Sunday I let him play in the yard a little while, even. Monday he seemed a little sick but I was not anxious. Tuesday I sent for the doctor fearing that he had intermittent fever. This we broke up with quinine, which he took very well. Tuesday night and Wednesday he had fever and every moment was pain . . . Wednesday night his bowels were bad. The doctor considered him in such good condition, however, that he did not come Thursday. Friday he discovered that he was threatened with bronchitis . . . His fever was entirely gone by Tuesday morning, but alas he showed symptoms of brain trouble. His cough was loose and his chest much better, and his bowels a little checked.
>
> I agonized that whole week in prayer. God made me willing to give him up, but oh I could not see him suffer though they tell me he was unconscious. He was dying two whole days and a night and a half, our darling!
>
> Miss Emma wouldn't leave him at all, she was stiff with holding him—he lay on the bed only the last day. He took his milk up to the last and his medicines and he passed away like a dream, our beautiful boy! No struggle, not even a hard breath!
>
> Dear old Doctor would come in and say, "Poor little John!" He couldn't bear to see him suffer. Wednesday night or Thursday morning rather, Mrs. Rogers and Miss Emma and I bathed his little dimpled limbs and wax-like features and dressed him

in the little blue dress that came to Ermine from Aunt Alice
with Miss Hammon's embroidery on it, and laid him away in
his white carriage to await his little coffin. When it came we
fairly surrounded him with flowers. He looked to me just like
sister Sallie.

He was the pet of the church and the neighborhood—no
one ever saw him except to admire the rosy big boy! All the
church members came who could, and they clubbed together
and hired carriages and went out to the grave. There were in
all eight carriages. The Methodist missionaries came and even
helped nurse him and Mr. and Mrs. Rogers, Presbyterian
neighbors, took our children to their house to sleep the two
last nights and came themselves and stayed with us. Mr.
Rogers didn't go to bed for two nights.

At five o'clock we sang a song in English and then in Portuguese and had reading and prayer in both and then our Baby
was taken to the lovely Caju Cemetery . . . Over his little body,
still in death, I had the opportunity of explaining to several
neighbors the plan of salvation and I believe that his death will
be the means of bringing not a few to Jesus.

I think his papa nursed him more than he had ever done
one of his babes and he has lost several pounds in the last few
days of anxiety and wakefulness he has spent with him. I'll
have so much time now. I'll be so lonely . . . Five years ago
Luther went away. If only I could forget the last few hours of
suffering and remember only his bright beautiful little life of
fourteen months, then I could be happy again.[24]

She added:

Our precious little John is safe, so safe, but I miss his precious
little happy life so much that I would glad join him if I could.
It seems to me that Heaven is growing rich for me! When Pa
and Ma go I'll have little here to claim my life . . . oh, I am so
sad since baby went.[25]

OLIVER HALBERT BAGBY

Oliver was born on August 25, 1893, in Waco, Texas, while
the Bagbys were on furlough. He acquired his elementary and
high school education at the Girls' School of Sao Paulo, and re-

turned to the United States for his undergraduate studies. Will wrote Willingham, requesting that someone look after Oliver while he attended Richmond College in Virginia. Oliver enjoyed giving lectures on Brazil to churches in the area and was a popular speaker.[26]

After graduating from Richmond College, Oliver studied medicine at Galveston with the thought of becoming a self-supporting medical missionary in Brazil. He also enlisted in the military service and participated in training exercises during World War I. The war ended, however, before he was sent to fight overseas. A year away from graduation at Galveston Medical College, he walked away from the school campus on February 19, 1919, leaving two trunks of personal belongings neatly packed: "His fraternity pin and his college ring were in the trunks, and he left a note on top of the two trunks saying, 'Keep till called for.'"[27] Will and Anne had sent him money for his return to Brazil, and he used it apparently to start a new life.[28] The death of Z. C. Taylor in the great hurricane at Galveston, Texas, may have prompted Oliver's departure.

The Bagbys were heartbroken and asked the corresponding secretary of the Foreign Mission Board to advertise Oliver's disappearance in the denominational papers. The secretary responded that advertising in the denominational papers would probably have no effect. A similar incident had befallen John Lowe, missionary to China, a few years earlier and his son had returned after two years. Oliver would probably do the same.[29]

The Bagbys hired a private investigator to find Oliver but without success. Will took an unapproved furlough to the United States in 1925 with information that someone had seen Oliver in San Antonio two years earlier. The trip yielded nothing but more heartache. Years later, the Bagbys believed that Oliver sent a package from Melbourne, Australia, but they never heard from their son after his disappearance.[30]

ALICE ANNE BAGBY SMITH

Alice Anne Bagby was born on June 20, 1896, in Rio de Janeiro. As a child, she suffered from rheumatic trouble, a problem which required sea baths in Santos. One such visit lasted five weeks and cost the Bagbys $200. She received her preparatory education at the Girls' School of Sao Paulo and MacKenzie College in Sao Paulo.[31] Alice entered Baylor College for Women in 1914 and graduated in 1918. She received a missionary degree from the Fort Worth training school in 1920. The Bagby women made quite an impression in Texas while attending school. Will wrote laughingly, "Am now introduced as the 'father of Alice and Helen Bagby!' Such fame!"[32]

Will asked the board to send Alice to help her mother with the Sao Paulo school after graduation, but Anne wrote Ray saying her daughter was too young for the job. The board appointed Alice to the Sao Paulo school in 1921. In the meantime, however, Alice had fallen in love with Harley Smith, a graduate of Howard Payne University in Brownwood, Texas. Harley and Alice decided to marry and seek appointment to Brazil together. The board appointed them as missionaries to Brazil in 1923.[33]

HELEN EDNA BAGBY HARRISON

Helen Edna Bagby was born on August 13, 1900, in Rio de Janeiro. She received her education at the Girls' School of Sao Paulo and MacKenzie College in Sao Paulo. Her first music teacher was Roxy Grove.[34] Helen attended Baylor College for Women and completed a double major in English and music in 1919. She earned a degree from the missionary training school in Fort Worth in 1921 through financial aid supplied by the Margaret Fund. Helen was engaged to be married while attending the training school, but her fiancee, Mr. Jeffery, broke the engagement and her heart.[35]

The Foreign Mission Board appointed Helen as a missionary in 1923. Will asked the board to let her do general women's work, Sunday School superintending, and visiting in Sao Paulo when she returned to Brazil as a missionary.[36] Dr. Ray, corresponding secretary of the Foreign Mission Board, answered that he did not believe it wise to "pile up kinfolk in the same station," so the board selected Helen to serve at the Rio mission.[37] As a compromise, Will requested that Helen return to the Sao Paulo mission for a year to rest, after which she could decide which field she wished to occupy.[38] Ray countered that they needed Helen badly in the Rio College and that he expected the Bagbys to "do the sacrificial thing" and make her go.[39] Helen remained in Sao Paulo.

Helen moved to Porto Alegre in 1928 to help Harley and Alice with the boarding school.[40] She served as principal of the school in Porto Alegre from 1928 to 1939. The board was forced to make personnel cuts due to the depression in 1929 and asked Helen to resign. She continued her work, however, supported by First Baptist Church, Ponca City, Oklahoma, for several years, and the board reappointed her in 1935. She married Dr. W. C. Harrison in 1939, a few months before her father's death.[41] Helen became the chief archivist for the family papers and wrote *The Bagbys of Brazil* as a tribute to the work of her mother and father. Unfortunately, she also purged the family papers of any letters which might have cast an unfavorable light on the Bagby legacy.

ALBERT IAN BAGBY

Albert Ian Bagby was born on July 26, 1903 and bore a remarkable resemblance to his father. He too received his education at the Girls' School of Sao Paulo. He visited the United States with his parents on their 1919 furlough and stayed in missionary housing at Southwestern Baptist Theological Seminary. Albert accompanied his father on preaching engagements and often played the piano for churches where William Bagby preached.[42] Albert attended Baylor University and furthered his education with a degree from Southern Seminary. The seminary celebrated his arrival because he was the seven thousandth student to matriculate.[43]

While in Brazil, Albert took piano from Sr. Manfredini who declared him a prodigy. He continued his music studies under Buhler in Paris and returned to Brazil to help in the music department of the school at Porto Alegre. He taught piano, theory, and harmony. Albert hoped to begin a concert career, but that dream never took form. He "plunged into evangelistic work" in a poorer section of Porto Alegre and was the superintendent of the Sunday School at the Floresta church. He later married Thelma Frith.[44]

THE SCHOOL AT PORTO ALEGRE

Harley and Alice Bagby Smith left for Brazil after their appointment as Southern Baptist missionaries on September 18, 1924. After eight months of language study in Rio de Janeiro, Harley traveled to Rio Grande do Sul to conduct revival meetings. His trip included preaching in four evangelistic crusades and singing in three others. He baptized four candidates, helped in the organization of one church, and helped ordain three deacons.[45]

The South Brazil Mission assigned Harley to Rio College, but he declined the assignment after consulting with Will. The results in Rio Grande do Sul compelled him to that field. It appeared a Bagby son-in-law could choose whichever field he wanted. Mr. and Mrs. Pettigrew met Harley and Alice when they arrived in Porto Alegre. The Smiths began to teach English classes at once because so many church members were illiterate.[46]

Harley and Alice organized the Baptist school at Porto Alegre as a private institution in 1926. They named the school the *Colegio Batista Americano,* and "winning souls" was the foremost reason for its founding.[47] They publicized the opening of their Baptist school in the newspapers and employed a carpenter to build ten desks. Because Harley still knew little Portuguese, Alice not only enrolled new students but also taught five hours a day. Harley taught English classes eight to ten hours a day, sometimes until 10:30 in the evening, to cover school expenses. The school also helped national Baptists by conducting a Bible school for ministerial students and lay workers. Along with his teaching duties, Harley served as corresponding secretary of the Rio Grande do Sul mission.[48]

The school was immediately successful and matriculated 267 students in 1926, although Alice would have considered thirty scholars a success. Classes included English, typewriting, and bookkeeping. The enrollment increased to 330 in 1927, 393 in 1928, and 419 in 1929. New classes were added, such as

Latin, French, Italian, German, Portuguese, shorthand, arithmetic, law, and composition. Music classes included violin, flute,
theory, harmony, piano, and voice. The government offered
financial aid, which Harley and Alice refused because of their
Baptist principles.[49]

The Porto Alegre school became the official typewriting
school of one of the wealthiest firms in Rio Grande do Sul,
Bromberg and Co. The company furnished typewriters and kept
them repaired at no charge. They granted students of the school
half-fare on the city street cars, a privilege usually allowed to students of governmental schools only.[50]

After their 1927 furlough William and Anne Bagby joined
Harley and Alice in Porto Alegre to help with the school. It faced
serious financial difficulties although it was prospering numerically. Both the Smiths and Bagbys solicited funds to keep the
school in operation. Alice wrote several churches and women's
groups asking them to send five dollars a month as loans which
they would repay in the future. A pastor from Galveston, Texas,
A. A. Sanders, contacted William Bagby and agreed to give
$20,000 toward the school. The funds would be divided $10,000
for the land, and $10,000 for the building. Bagby related, "He
readily and heartily accepted my suggestion that the whole
property should be in your and his names and not in the name
of the Board or South Brazil Mission, or any Association, or organization so that you and he can always control it, and use it as
you please."[51] Sanders planned to go to Porto Alegre with his
wife to help in the school, but failed to provide the promised
funds for the school or make the trip.

When Harley and Alice Bagby Smith went on furlough in
1932, they were unable to return because of financial difficulties
at the Foreign Mission Board after the Seventy-Five Million Dollar campaign. They were kept on indefinite furlough without
salary.[52] William Bagby wrote Maddry, corresponding secretary
of the Foreign Mission Board:

> This is an S.O.S. call if there ever was one and may God help
> us! I am at the end of my life in sore need of immediate relief
> as your sole male missionary in nine-tenths of the State. . . . If
> Harley Smith and wife do not come back at once, it seems to
> me that all is lost . . . For God's sake send them at once. We

cannot wait . . . Send Alice and Harley without delay now, now.
God grant it.[53]

Harley and Alice returned in 1934. After struggling for several years financially, the school asked the South Brazil Mission to take ownership. After the Smiths resigned as missionaries of the board in 1942, Dr. W. C. and Helen Bagby Harrison supervised the school with the help of Albert Bagby and his wife. The institution became a standard Brazilian high school.[54]

CONFLICT ON THE FIELD

Contention between missionaries A. L. Dunstan and Harley Smith was the main reason the elder Bagbys moved to Porto Alegre after their furlough in 1927. William and Anne Bagby's presence on the Rio Grande do Sul field only exacerbated the situation. The crisis was emotionally charged on both sides and never reconciled, although Dunstan and Bagby previously had served many years together on the Brazilian field.

The board stationed A. L. Dunstan at Campos initially. He quickly encountered persecution and became discouraged, so the board requested that Dunstan be moved to the station at Espiritu Santo. However, the situation improved at Campos and he remained there. Bagby wrote the board saying, "Dunstan is a good man, and on the right field for him, would do an excellent and solid work."[55]

Dunstan served on several important committees with William Bagby. The South Brazil Mission appointed him to the first executive committee of the Baptist Publication Society. He was also selected as one of the first trustees of the college and seminary at Rio de Janeiro. A rift between the two men developed, however, over chartering the new institutions according to Brazilian law. Missionaries Dunstan and Crosland attempted to block ratification of the charters. William Bagby asked the board to ignore their opposition because neither had done any school work in Brazil. The board endorsed William Bagby's counsel and the charters.[56]

Dunstan requested a move to Santos in 1908 to begin a new work, but the board assigned him to the Sao Paulo station instead. Dunstan and Bagby worked together at Santos, Jundiahy, and Alto de Serra. Bagby wrote the Foreign Mission Board in April 1910 asking them to take over the Girls' School of Sao Paulo and elect a board of trustees from the Sao Paulo mission. He recommended missionaries Deter and Dunstan for the position.[57]

Earlier in 1910, the Foreign Mission Board approved a move for Dunstan to the state of Rio Grande do Sul. Dunstan moved to Rio Grande do Sul in 1911 and began work in Porto Alegre. He organized the local mission that year and by 1916 established seven churches. The population in Porto Alegre exploded to 408,728 by 1925 because of immigration. The geography of Rio Grande do Sul was much like that of Texas.[58]

When Harley Smith selected Rio Grande do Sul as a mission site, it was with the permission of A. L. Dunstan. Controversy erupted quickly, however, when Harley, treasurer for the mission, accused Dunstan of misappropriating rent money.[59]

Contention between Smith and Dunstan escalated when the South Brazil Mission considered removing support from Dunstan's school in Pelotas and giving it to the school at Porto Alegre. The board did not wish to duplicate schools, or set up a rivalry in the state. They requested that the South Brazil Mission appoint a committee to decide the best location for a school in the state of Rio Grande do Sul. The committee's recommendation to move support to the school in Porto Alegre angered Dunstan.[60]

Dunstan was on furlough in the United States, but he wrote missionaries in Rio Grande do Sul that he was going to move to Porto Alegre when he returned in order to set up an alternative school. The committee from the South Brazil Mission then voted in favor of Dunstan's plan. Their action caused Harley to reply, "What are we coming to? They are treating us like children who do not know what we want or what is best for our work!"[61] Ultimately, the committee decided to keep the school in Pelotas with Dunstan as director. The committee believed that without proper funding the Porto Alegre school would be forced to close. Anne wrote Alice:

> It looks to me as though you and Harley will be called upon to fight alone just as we had to do—we never had substantial help

from the Board or a proper school building until twenty years after we began ours. It needs titanic patience and work to build up a school without money. May God help you![62]

The plan was to reopen the school later when the ill feelings between Smith and Dunstan had passed. Anne Bagby wrote to Alice, "But they did not know the Smith and Bagby material, did they, child?"[63]

Will and Anne Bagby were also on furlough at the time, but they wrote Harley and Alice promising they would join them in Porto Alegre as reinforcements. Helen and Albert Bagby soon followed.[64] Will Bagby wrote words of encouragement to Alice:

> Don't attach too much importance to Dunstan's threats. I know him of old, and do not fear much. I firmly believe that your school is doing God's will and that it has a great future. Dunstan cannot stop it, nor greatly hurt it. I do not doubt his evil intentions, but he has never been able to effect any permanent harm anywhere, nor any great good![65]

The conflict spread to the Rio mission when a missionary wrote A. C. Duggar an anonymous note. It falsely reported that the Bagbys were trying to get Duggar removed from the field:

> There is a move on foot to have you dismissed from the service of our Board as missionary. Those whom you think to be your best friends, are those who will initiate the campaign for your dismissal. You had better take the warning from one who knows, and not despise the friendship of the most solid man the Board has in Brazil — I refer to Bro. Dunstan — giving preference to the other missionaries in your state. I should not wonder if the campaign against you did not begin here in Rio when Dr. Bagby was here: and as his company made an effort to have Bro. Dunstan dismissed, so will they make a greater effort against you. You have made great mistakes there: but you can overcome them all, if you will take the counsel of a man who sees things as they are.[66]

The unidentified missionary said, "You had better make a friend of Dunstan instead of that other group in Rio Grande do Sul."[67] The Duggars were forced to resign several months later, but they left for the United States supporting the Bagbys.[68]

A. L. Dunstan, along with a group of pastors in the Porto Alegre field, submitted eleven resolutions against the Smiths and Bagbys to the Foreign Mission Board in 1930:

First: Since the work passed out of the hands of Brother Dunstan, it has been slowly on the decline.

Second: The Rev. Smith is very heavily in debt and the funds which should go to evangelization, go to pay off personal debts. According to information given us, there is a debt of sixteen thousand milreis on a printing outfit which is not functioning at present. He himself confessed that there is a debt of eight thousand milreis on his school.

Third: The Rev. Smith recently announced his departure for the United States, declaring that the work will continue to function under the supervision of Miss Helen Bagby. Since she is not a missionary of our Board, it appears to us to be wrong to leave her in charge of the work. Furthermore, it seems to us that they plan for Dr. Bagby to receive the funds, which come for the aid of the churches, and deliver them to Miss Helen for the liquidation of debts.

Fourth: The properties pertaining to the churches are in a deplorable state of repair.

Fifth: The churches have reached the point where they will no longer subject themselves to the directorship of the Revs. Smith and Bagby, nor Miss Helen. If the necessary steps are not taken . . . they will . . . seek help from other sources.

Sixth: Since the arrival in this State of Revs. Smith and Bagby, they have not ceased to ill-treat brother Dunstan. They call him "a demented old man" and . . . a liar, hypocrite, and deceiver. . . . They never lose an opportunity to molest him in his work and are constantly defaming him. This charge is strengthened by a letter which brother Dunstan holds, sent to the Board by the Revs. Smith and Bagby. Brother Dunstan has been in this State for twenty years. He has given us an example of Christian conduct and established a work that has done credit to him and to the cause of the Lord. While he directed, the cause prospered.

Seventh: The Revs. Smith and Bagby have lately tried to sell the properties of the churches of this city and use the money for the erection of a school building.

Eighth: Especially Mr. Smith with his wife have shown a profound dislike for the most humble of our brethren. . . . One of our Churches to them is composed of "soldiers and Negroes" and another to "a handful of fools." . . . Such sayings as "we did not come to evangelize Negroes" has wounded profoundly the hearts of our brethren. The wound cannot be healed as long as they remain in this State.

Ninth: The private life at the home of Messrs. Smith and Bagby has been a scandal to all who know them. Due to them, Baptists are held to be worse than non-believers. They openly make anti-Christian feasts, rent picture shows and theaters, advertise themselves the best actors of the city, and go on the stage to represent scenes (if not shameful) at least anti-biblical.

Tenth: The attitude of the above mentioned missionaries toward the churches is that of absolute ownership.

Eleventh: Due to the above mentioned facts, we come to you asking that they be withdrawn from the direction of the work of this state, and to send to us a direction in better conditions. We make no request as to whom that director may be, so long as he is of better character than the present directors.[69]

The accusations were half-truths, but they offer an intriguing glimpse into the relationship between Southern Baptist missionaries and Brazilian nationals during the period. Bagby wrote the executive committee of the South Brazil Mission denying all charges made against his clan. He asked the committee to work out a compromise for the work in Rio Grande do Sul.[70]

The Bagbys entreated the Foreign Mission Board to permit them to stay at Porto Alegre undisturbed and to bar Dunstan from interfering with their work.[71] Ray, corresponding secretary of the Foreign Mission Board, wrote William Bagby agreeing: "The suggestion is that Brother Dunstan confine his labors to the southern part of the State of Rio Grande do Sul, in the general region of Pelotas and Rio Grande: and that Brethren Bagby and Smith confine their labors to the northern part of the state with Porto Alegre as the center."[72] The dispute continued for several years, however, because Dunstan persisted in ministering to churches in the Porto Alegre area.

William Bagby harbored a deep animosity toward Dunstan until the end.[73] He wrote Anne, "Dunstan is either crazy, or not a Christian!"[74] Bagby wrote Ray, "Dunstan is no better than J. Frank Norris. . . . Your confidence in Dunstan and esteem for him are utterly misplaced and unfounded, and you cannot rely on any statement whatever which he makes regarding this field."[75]

William Bagby said he and Dunstan were irreconcilable, to which Ray replied, "just keep away from each other."[76] The conflict never abated and Ray wrote the Rio Grande do Sul missionaries asking permission to burn all correspondence concerning the controversy. Both William Buck Bagby and A. L. Dunstan agreed.[77] Bagby wrote in 1936 that Dunstan was still his "mortal enemy" and should be removed from the Rio Grande do Sul field. Dunstan's death in 1937 granted Bagby's request, and the conflict ceased.[78]

ELDER STATESMAN

Will and Anne spent the final years of their Brazilian ministry in Porto Alegre, Rio Grande do Sul, helping their daughter and son-in-law run the *Colegio Batista Americano*. The Bagbys chose the field for several reasons. First, the school was immediately successful, but the teaching load had overwhelmed Harley and Alice Bagby Smith. It took only four years for the school at Porto Alegre to achieve an enrollment equal to the Girls' School of Sao Paulo, the flagship Baptist school of Brazil. Will and Anne Bagby always gravitated toward new works that were achieving phenomenal results. Second, the Bagbys decided to buttress the Smiths in their conflict with missionary A. L. Dunstan. Unfortunately, they never resolved the controversy, which lead to Harley and Alice Bagby Smith's resignation from the Foreign Mission Board several years later. Clearly, the presence of William and Anne Bagby in Rio Grande do Sul hindered work on the field until both Dunstan and Bagby passed away.

In the midst of irreconcilable differences with missionary

Dunstan on the Rio Grande do Sul field, William and Anne Bagby enjoyed several Golden Jubilee celebrations during their twilight years of ministry in Brazil. Brazilian Baptists celebrated the Bagbys Golden Wedding Anniversary in October 1930. Then they celebrated the Golden Jubilee of Southern Baptist work in Brazil in January 1931. William Bagby wrote: "These have been years of marvelous experiences of God's grace, and love, and monstrous leadings, and our hearts are full of gratitude to Him for all his mercies and providence."[79] First Baptist Church, Rio de Janeiro, celebrated its Golden Jubilee in 1934.[80]

Missionary S. L. Watson chiefly organized and publicized the Latin-American Baptist Congress in 1930. Prominent guests came from Brazil, Uruguay, Argentina, Mexico, Cuba, and Chile. J. H. Rushmore, president of the World alliance, T. B. Ray, corresponding secretary of the Foreign Mission Board, and George W. Truett, pastor of First Baptist Church, Dallas, Texas, spoke at the meeting. William Bagby gave the keynote address.[81]

In his address to the Latin American Baptist Congress in 1930, William Bagby cited several reasons for the explosive growth of Southern Baptists in Brazil. First, the idea of democracy was "a new doctrine for the underprivileged in a Catholic society largely dominated by paternalistic and feudalistic ideals."[82] The missionaries sought to give every individual dignity and worth, no matter their economic standing. Second, Southern Baptist evangelism involved the conversion of the whole person, and the transformation of every facet of the believer's life. Southern Baptist missionaries felt a deep responsibility "not only to lead people to a personal acceptance of Christ, but also to inspire them with the beauty and glory of Christian fellowship and service."[83] Third, Southern Baptists publicly preached the gospel and demanded that their converts follow "the New Testament doctrine of a regenerated membership, which demanded the separation of the church from the world."[84]

Will and Anne Bagby were forced to return on furlough to the United States in 1935 because of health problems. They received surgical care at the Baptist Hospital in Dallas, Texas. Dr. Edgar Dunstan, director of the hospital and eldest son of missionary A. L. Dunstan, graciously superintended their visit. During their recovery, the couple stayed in a home provided by First Baptist Church, Dallas, Texas.[85]

The Bagbys returned to Brazil in 1936, although funds were short at the Foreign Mission Board because of the depression. William Bagby passed away in "The Land of the Southern Cross" on August 5, 1939, after a short illness of bronchial pneumonia. His daughter, Ermine, contracted the same illness and died two weeks later. Will was laid to rest in the Baptist cemetery in Porto Alegre. Anne followed him on December 22, 1942, and was buried in the British cemetery at Recife, a thousand miles away from her husband.[86] It is fitting that in both life and death they occupied north and south Brazil. Their life and ministry spanned the entire country and left an enduring legacy. The Bagby children, and five generations following, continued the saga.

Chapter 8

Passionate Laborers
on a Fertile Field

. . . And though a man may not discover the elements of his greatness until he has passed from among them, still his name will be honored, and imperishable monuments will be erected to his memory long years after his departure.

— from a sermon by William Buck Bagby[1]

The results of Southern Baptist mission work in Brazil during the ministry of William Buck and Anne Luther Bagby were staggering. Ten years after they had been on the field, the Bagbys reported ten churches, 434 baptisms, and 419 members. At the time of Will's death in 1939, Southern Baptists had organized 778 churches, performed 47,114 baptisms, and 68,731 Brazilians had joined a Baptist church in Brazil. Significantly, most of the growth of Baptists in Brazil came in South Brazil, the area in which Will and Anne Bagby ministered.[2] Several factors contributed to their success.

Will and Anne planted an indigenous work in Brazil. After the revolution of 1889, Brazilians became very interested in American democracy. Baptist convictions about democratic church government were popular among Brazilians, and caused Baptist churches to grow rapidly. Freed from the domination of Catholic priests, Baptist converts enjoyed voicing their opinions about ecclesiastical affairs in church business meetings. The

Bagbys believed the change in political climate was divine providence. The combination of Brazilian openness to democracy and the gifts and abilities of Will and Anne Bagby clearly united to create a fertile field for harvest.

The churches continued to expand because Will stressed the importance of personal evangelism and tithing. One requirement for church membership was an agreement to share the gospel with family members. And the ratio of converts to members was remarkable in the early years of the South Brazil Mission. It was common for a Brazilian Baptist to lead five or six compatriots to Christ every year. From the beginning, Bagby emphasized the importance of Brazilian churches supporting themselves on the mission field. He further challenged the young Brazilian churches to look beyond their monetary needs and support foreign missions. The result was self-sufficient churches modeled after their organizer. The perseverence of spirit in the Bagbys lived on in the churches they established.

Will, the missionary organizer, orchestrated the work in a way that promoted growth. Z. C. Taylor believed in the importance of preaching the gospel and placed little significance on establishing churches until later in his ministry. Taylor also concentrated his efforts in the rural sections around Salvador, Bahia, instead of developing churches in major urban areas. Will, on the other hand, believed that they must organize churches, even with a small membership. He concentrated on the Brazilian cities that were experiencing explosive growth because of immigration. Bagby's plan led to the organization of thirty-seven Baptist churches, the first Baptist association, and the first Brazilian Baptist convention.

Brazilian leaders like F. F. Soren, Theodore Teixeira, and Tomaz da Costa provided the Bagbys with a vital link to their Brazilian constituency, and were another reason for the Bagbys success. Native workers served in important positions in the Brazilian Baptist convention. Soren became pastor of First Baptist Church, Rio de Janeiro, and president of the first Brazilian Baptist convention. Teixeira edited and published *O Jornal Batista,* the leading Brazilian Baptist denominational paper. Costa was an effective preacher in the states of Para, Minas Geraes, Bahia, and Sao Paulo.

Will used the persecution of Baptists in Brazil to strengthen the foreign mission cause in Brazil and the United States. Bagby pointed out to his Brazilian converts that persecution always followed believers in the New Testament. He asserted that the persecution Baptists faced in Brazil only proved that they were receiving the authentic gospel. Bagby encouraged editorial wars in the local newspapers because he recognized the value of free publicity. Newspapers in the United States published Bagby's letters about persecution by Catholic priests in Brazil because the letters fanned the flame of anti-Catholic bias emerging in the United States. And Bagby's writings served as proof of the Southern Baptist presence in a Catholic country. While on furlough, Will often raised funds for the Foreign Mission Board by capitalizing on the fear of Catholic immigration held by many Americans. His eloquent writing painted a picture in the mind of Texas Baptists that compelled them to sojourn to Brazil.

Without the "Texas Connection" the results in Brazil would have been sparse. Prominent Southern Baptist leaders in Texas like B. H. Carroll, A. T. Hawthorne, J. H. Luther, R. C. Burleson, R. C. Buckner, E. Y. Mullins, L. R. Scarborough, and George W. Truett supported the Bagbys in Brazil. Through the Anne Luther Societies, Baptist women in Texas exceeded their spouses in financial support for the mission cause in Brazil. Texas, however, sent more than money to the foreign field. Will and Anne used speaking engagements during their furloughs as effective recruitment meetings, and a steady stream of young men and women followed them to "The Land of the Southern Cross."

Important Southern Baptist leaders like B. H. Carroll and L. R. Scarborough sent their children to Brazil as missionaries. Baylor College for Women, Anne Bagby's alma mater, sent a greater percentage of graduates to the foreign mission field than any other Baptist college, and most went to Brazil. Texas began to support foreign missions like never before, and a partnership developed between Baptists in Brazil and Baptists in Texas that continues today. This partnership was unique in the history of the Foreign Mission Board. The Bagbys made a significant contribution to the mission emphasis at Southwestern Baptist Theological Seminary, Fort Worth, Texas. Because of B. H. Carroll's friendship with William and Anne Bagby, Southwestern Seminary has emphasized the training of missionaries from its beginning. The merger with the missionary training school for women furthered that vision. Southwestern Seminary has become the largest provider of trained men and women for the Southern Baptist Foreign Mission Board, due in a large part to the life and ministry of William Buck and Anne Luther Bagby in Brazil.

William was the chief organizer of Southern Baptist denominational work in Brazil. He organized the first church in Salvador, Bahia, on October 18, 1882. Bagby created the first Baptist association in Brazil on June 16, 1894, strongly influenced the establishment of the first Brazilian Baptist convention held on June 17, 1907, and served on four boards for the Brazilian Baptist convention during his tenure: Baptist Publishing House, Seminary Administration, Education, and Foreign Missions.[3] Brazilian Baptists also selected Bagby to commence foreign mission work in Chile. Indisputably the senior statesman of Baptists in Brazil, William addressed the first Latin American Baptist Conference in 1930 as the keynote speaker.

Anne Luther Bagby influenced women in Texas and Brazil, and she became a lightning rod for missions support. She helped Fannie Breedlove Davis promote and organize the first W.M.U. of Texas in 1880. Anne Bagby's departure to Brazil in 1881 served as a catalyst to the newly created organization. As a result, Baptist women in Texas increased their giving to foreign missions 850 percent during the first decade of Will and Anne's missionary service. In 1889 Anne also organized the first Brazilian W.M.U. in Rio de Janeiro, Brazil. During Anne Bagby's work in Sao Paulo, Baylor College for Women started the Anne Luther Bagby Scholarship Fund to give poor children an opportunity to receive a Baptist education. Anne Bagby supported the missionary training school movement among women in Texas against Annie Armstrong's wishes. She also developed a plan for a scholarship program at the missionary training school in Fort Worth, Texas.

William and Anne Bagby influenced Brazilian Baptists by emphasizing the importance of educational work in the evangelistic outreach of the Brazilian mission. The Bagbys founded the Girls' School of Sao Paulo, not only to teach their own children but also to reach the higher classes in Sao Paulo City with the gospel. The Girls' School of Sao Paulo became the flagship of Baptist work in Brazil and trained kindergarten teachers for schools throughout the country. Will inaugurated the call for a college and seminary on the Brazilian field. He wrote the Foreign Mission Board almost a decade before they established a college and seminary in Brazil, pleading for ministerial training. The board decided to locate the schools in Rio de Janeiro because of Bagby's counsel. Even in the twilight years of their ministry, William Buck and Anne Luther Bagby moved to Porto Alegre, Rio Grande do Sul, to help their daughter and son-in-law with a school founded "to win souls." Throughout their career, William and Anne Bagby stressed the importance of education as an evangelistic tool, a chief characteristic of Southern Baptist mission work in Brazil.

William and Anne Bagby personified the missionary spirit to an entire generation of Texans. They were rugged, individualistic, resolute, and uncompromising. Bringing the gospel to a foreign land demanded nothing less. Unfortunately, those same characteristics brought division and schism at the end of their ministry. Their legacy, however, is extraordinary. No missionary couple in the history of the Southern Baptist Foreign Mission Board has ever attained the level of spiritual fruitfulness achieved in the life and ministry of William Buck and Anne Luther Bagby.

Notes

Chapter 1

1. The source material for Anne Luther Bagby's early life is from the "Autobiography of Mrs. Anne Luther Bagby," in Tupper, *Decade*, 164-65; Harrison, *Bagbys of Brazil;* and John Hill Luther, "Autobiography, 1896," AMs [photocopy], Archives, Townsend Memorial Library, University of Mary Hardin-Baylor, Texas (hereafter cited as MHC).

2. Luther, "Autobiography," 35-36, MHC.

3. *Ibid.*

4. *Ibid.*

5. Anne to William's Mother, December 24, 1879, FWC.

6. Harrison, "Memoirs," 3.

7. Luther, "Autobiography," 39, MHC.

8. Harrison, *Bagbys of Brazil*, 8.

9. Anne to William's Mother, December 24, 1879, FWC.

10. Tupper, *Decade*, 164.

11. Luther, "Autobiography," 42.

12. Harrison, *Bagbys of Brazil*, 11.

13. Luther, "Autobiography," 49, MHC.

14. Anne to William, April 2, 1879, FWC.

15. Lois Smith Murray, *Baylor at Independence* (Waco, TX: Baylor University Press, 1972), 370-75.

16. *Ibid.*, 306.

17. Anne to William, October 11, 1878, FWC.

18. Harrison, *Bagbys of Brazil*, 13.

19. Anne to William, October 21, 1878, May 2, 1879, May 14, 1879, FWC.

20. Anne to William, October 21, 1878, FWC.

21. William to Anne, August 4, 1880, FWC.

22. The biographical information on William Buck and Anne Luther Bagby is based on a compilation of several source documents including: William Buck and Anne Luther Bagby, "Bagby-Luther Family Papers," Archives, A. Webb Roberts Library, Southwestern Baptist Theological Seminary, Fort Worth, Texas (hereafter cited as FWC); W. B. Bagby, "After Fifty Years," *Texas Baptist Standard*, September 24, 1931, 1; Helen Bagby Harrison, "William Buck Bagby," *Baylor Bulletin*, June 1928, 5; *Ibid.*, "William Buck Bagby," in *Ten Men From Baylor* ed. J. M. Price (Kansas City: Central Seminary Press, 1945); id., *The Bagbys in Brazil* (Nashville: Broadman Press, 1954); A. R. Crabtree, "The Missionary Organizer," FWC; P. G. Vining, "Adventure in the Land of Today and

Tomorrow," *Texas Baptist Standard,* June 9, 1927, 1; *Ibid.,* "Fifty Years in Brazil: Dr. and Mrs. W. B. Bagby in Brazil," *The Baylor Monthly,* February 1931, 3; H. A. Tupper, *A Decade of Foreign Missions: 1880-1890* (Richmond, Virginia: Foreign Mission Board of the Southern Baptist Convention, 1891).

23. Harrison, *Ten Men,* 14-15.

24. Harrison, *Bagbys of Brazil,* 2.

25. William to Sister Ermine, September 27, 1890, FWC.

26. Vining, "Adventures," 1.

27. *Ibid.*

28. Helen Baldwin, "*Bagbys of Brazil:* Continue Remarkable Missionary Work" *Waco Tribune Herald* (May 24, 1959): 1. Waco residents named the streets "Bagby" and "Mary."

29. Harrison, "Baylor Bulletin," 1.

30. Helen Bagby Harrison, "Oral Memoirs of Helen Bagby Harrison," interview by William Pitts, Jr. (Waco, TX: Baylor University Institute of Oral History, 1979): 4.

31. Harrison, *Bagbys of Brazil,* 3.

32. Z. C. Taylor, "The Rise and Progress of Baptist Missions in Brazil: An Autobiography, 1916," TMs [photocopy], p. 2-7, Texas Collection, University of Baylor, Waco, Texas (hereafter cited as BUC).

33. Harrison, "Memoirs," 4.

34. Vining, "Adventures," 2.

35. W. B. Bagby, "License to Preach," ADS, May 5, 1877, FWC.

36. C. E. Evans, *The Story of Texas Schools* (Austin, TX: The Steck Company, 1955), 99.

37. William to Mother, November 30, 1877, FWC.

38. William to Mother, January 4, 1878, FWC.

39. *Ibid.*

40. Anne to William, September 28, 1878, FWC.

41. Harrison, *Bagbys of Brazil,* 10-11.

42. Anne to William, August 6, 1878, FWC.

43. *Ibid.*

44. Anne to William, September 28, 1878, FWC.

45. Anne to William, January 19, 1879, FWC.

46. Taylor, "Rise and Progress," 12-17.

47. Anne to William, March 6; March 29, 1879, FWC.

48. Anne to William, March 8, 1879, FWC.

49. Anne to William, July 2, 1879, FWC.

50. Anne to William, June 13, 1879, FWC.

51. Anne to William, July 28, 1979, FWC.

52. Anne to William, March 28, 1879, FWC.

53. Anne to William, February 22; March 8, 1879, FWC.

54. Harrison, *Bagbys of Brazil,* 17.

55. Anne to William, February 15, 1880, FWC.

56. Anne to William, October 8, 1879, FWC.

57. Anne to William, April 11, 1880, FWC.

58. Anne to William, February 15, 1880; January 22, 1881, FWC.

59. Anne to Will, February 8, 1880, FWC.

60. Anne to Will, February 22, 1880, FWC.

Chapter 2

1. David Carson Davis, "Thomas Jefferson Bowen and His Plans for the Redemption of Africa" (M.A. thesis, Baylor University, 1978), 115.

2. Harrison, *Bagbys of Brazil*, 19.

3. Davis, "Bowen," 102.

4. Davis, "Bowen," 105.

5. *Ibid.*

6. *Ibid.*, 102.

7. *Ibid.*, 105.

8. C. C. Andrews, *Brazil: Its Conditions and Prospects* (New York: D. Appleton and Company, 1887), 116.

9. David Gueiros Vieira, "Protestantism and the Religious Question in Brazil, 1850-1875" (Ph.D. diss., The American University, 1972), 537.

10. Lawrence F. Hill, "The Confederate Exodus to Latin America" *The Southern Historical Quarterly* 34 (October 1935): 100-34; (January 1936): 161-99; and (April 1936): 309-26.

11. Hill, "Confederate Exodus," (January 1936): 192.

12. Lawrence F. Hill, "Confederate Exiles in Brazil" *Hispanic American Historical Review* 7 (May 1927): 192-210.

13. Hill, "Confederate Exodus," (October 1935): 107.

14. Hill, "Confederate Exodus," (January 1927): 195.

15. Hill, "Confederate Exodus," (October 1935): 119.

16. *Ibid.*

17. Hill, "Confederate Exodus," (April 1936): 310.

18. James E. Bear, *Mission to Brazil* (New York: Board of World Missions, Presbyterian Church United States, 1961), 5.

19. Hill, "Confederate Exodus," (October 1935): 106.

20. Hill, "Confederate Exodus," (January 1936): 162.

21. H. A. Tupper, *The Foreign Missions of the Southern Baptist Convention* (Richmond: Foreign Mission Board of the Southern Baptist Convention, 1886), 10; William Buck Bagby, "Annual Report—Brazilian Mission," April 30, 1885, Southern Baptist Library and Archives, Nashville, Tennessee (hereafter cited as NTC).

22. William R. Estep, *Whole Gospel Whole World* (Nashville: Broadman and Holman, 1994), 126.

23. Tupper, *Foreign Missions*, 10.

24. Tupper, *Foreign Missions*, 12.

25. *Ibid.*

26. Mary E. Wright, *The Missionary Work of the Southern Baptist Convention* (Philadelphia: American Baptist Publication Society, 1902), 213.

27. Harrison, *Bagbys of Brazil*, 20.

28. Betty Antunes de Oliveira, *North American Imigration to Brazil: Tombstone Recordes of the Campo Cemetery* (Rio de Janeiro: By the author, 1978), 30.

29. Ratcliff to Tupper, October 1, 1878, NTC.

30. J. M. Carroll, *A History of Texas Baptists: Comprising a Detailed Account of Their Activities, Their Progress, and Their Achievements* (Dallas, TX: Baptist Standard Publishing, 1923), 599; Wright, Missionary Work, 213.

31. William to Tupper, May 15, 1881, NTC.

32. Charles E. Maddry, *Christ's Expendables* (Nashville: Broadman Press, 1949), 8.

33. Anne to William, July 1, 1879, FWC.

34. Taylor, "Rise and Progress," 12.

35. A. R. Crabtree, *Baptists in Brazil: A History of Southern Baptist's Greatest Mission Field* (Rio de Janeiro: Baptist Publishing House, 1953), 36.

36. *Ibid.*

37. Anne to William, June 11, 1880, FWC.

38. Anne to William, June 19, 1880, FWC.

39. Anne to William, July 5, 1880, FWC.

40. William to Sister Ermine, July 15, 1880, FWC.

41. Anne to William, July 16, 1880, FWC.

42. William to Sister Ermine, July 16, 1880, FWC.

43. William to Anne, July 17, 1880, FWC.

44. William to Anne, August 20, 1880, FWC.

45. William to Anne, August 8, 1880, FWC.

46. William to Anne, August14; August 18, 1880, FWC.

47. William to Anne, August 30, 1880, FWC.

48. William to Anne, September 8, 1880, FWC.

49. Anne to William, October 7, 1880, FWC.

50. W. B. Bagby, "Marriage License," October 22, 1880, FWC.

51. Taylor, "Rise and Progress," 11.

52. Martin, "Hidden Work," 106.

53. Alma Hunt, *History of Women's Training Union* (Nashville: Convention Press, 1964), 18. Fannie Breedlove Davis served as president of the Texas W.M.U. for fifteen years and also served on the committee that organized the Southern Baptist Convention W.M.U. in 1888.

54. Harrison, "Memoirs," 7.

55. Copass, *Women and Their Work*, 210-36.

56. Smith, *Centennial History*, 39.

57. Martin, "Hidden Work," 114; Copass, *Women and Their Work*, 209; Smith, *Baptist Women of Texas*, 156.

58. Harrison, "Memoirs," 7.

59. William to Anne, August 24; September 16; September 20; October 17, 1880, FWC.

60. William to Mother, November 1, 1880, FWC.

61. Anne to William's Mother, December 7, 1880, FWC.

62. Anne to Ermine, December 23, 1880, FWC.

63. Anne to Father, January 14, 1881, FWC.

64. William to Texas Baptists, January 15, 1881, FWC.

65. Harrison, "Memoirs," 7.

66. Anne Bagby, "Diary," January 17, 1881, FWC.

67. *Ibid.*, February 7, 1881, FWC.

68. Anne to Mother, February 19, 1881, FWC.

69. Anne Bagby, "Diary," March 18, 1881, FWC.

70. *Ibid.*, February 28, 1881, FWC.

71. *Ibid.*, March 2, 1881, FWC.

Chapter 3

1. Anne to Father, May 21, 1881, FWC.
2. Jan Knippers Black, "Historical Setting" in *Brazil: A Country Study*, ed. Richard Nyrop (Washington, D.C.: Headquarters, Department of the Army, 1982), 6-24; M. G. White and H. H. Muirhead, *In the Land of the Southern Cross* (Richmond: Foreign Mission Board Educational Department, 1929), 2.
3. Thomas Lynn Smith, *Brazil: Portrait of Half a Continent* (New York: Dryden Press, 1951), 39.
4. Black, "Historical Setting," 10.
5. *Ibid.*, 16.
6. *Ibid.*, 18.
7. *Ibid.*, 20.
8. *Ibid.*
9. *Ibid.*
10. Smith, *Portrait*, 40.
11. *Ibid.*
12. *Ibid.*, 24.
13. Harrison, *Bagbys of Brazil*, 44.
14. William to Hawthorne, March 19, 1881, FWC.
15. William to Mother, March 8, 1881, FWC.
16. William to Tupper, March 12, 1881, NTC.
17. William to Tupper, March 31, 1881, NTC.
18. William to Mother, March 8, 1881, FWC.
19. W. B. Bagby, "Letter," *Foreign Mission Journal* 12 (March 1881): 4.
20. William to Tupper, March 21, 1881, FWC.
21. Anne to Parents, March 20, 1881, FWC.
22. Anne to Father, May 1, 1881; Anne to Parents, July 17, 1881, FWC.
23. Anne Bagby, "Diary," January 22, 1882, FWC.
24. Anne to Parents, March 20, 1881, FWC.
25. Anne to Parents, March 20, 1881, FWC.
26. William to Anne's Mother, April 1, 1881, FWC; Bertoldo Gatz, "Ministerial Training For Baptist Churches in the State of Sao Paulo, Brazil" (D.Min. thesis, Fuller Theological Seminary, 1989), 61. This school was the first educational institution established in South America by evangelical missionaries.
27. H. H. Muirhead, "Evangelical Christianity in Brazil During the Colonial and Imperial Periods, 1500-1889" (Th.D. diss., Southwestern Baptist Theological Seminary, 1923), 91; Bear, *Mission to Brazil*, 17.
28. Anne to Father, November 1, 1881, FWC.
29. William to Dr. Luther, October 4, 1881, FWC.
30. William to Mother, November 10, 1881, FWC.
31. Anne to Mother, November 21, 1881, FWC.
32. William to Foreign Mission Board (FMB), June 12, 1881; William to Tupper, March 12, 1881; May 31, 1881, NTC. The Station church was a split from the Santa Barbara church that formed a few months before the Bagbys landed in Brazil, leaving both churches financially destitute.
33. William to Sister Ermine, September 6,. 1881, FWC.
34. *Ibid.*; William to Tupper, October 26, 1881, NTC.

35. William to Tupper, March 21, 1881, FWC.

36. Harrison, *Bagbys of Brazil*, 53. Kate Crawford Taylor was a schoolteacher from Salado, Texas, and niece of China missionary T. P. Crawford.

37. William to Dr. Luther, April 26, 1882, FWC; W. B. Bagby, "Annual Report," 29 April 1882, NTC.

38. Taylor to Hawthorne, August 20, 1882, BUC.

39. W. B. Bagby, "Letter," *Foreign Mission Journal* 14 (October 1882): 159.

40. Taylor to Hawthorne, August 20, 1882, BUC.

41. Anne to the Anne Luther Societies, June 21, 1882, FWC.

42. Anne to Parents, June 5, 1881, FWC.

43. Anne to Parents, July 17, 1881, FWC.

44. Committee on South American Missions (COSAM), "Minutes," November 6, 1882, Archives, Foreign Mission Board, Southern Baptist Convention, Richmond, Virginia (hereafter cited as RVC); Anne to Tupper, July 28, 1882, NTC; Anne to Mother, April 24, 1882, FWC.

45. William to Tupper, March 31, 1881, NTC.

46. Taylor, "Rise and Progress," 11.

47. Hawthorne to Anne, July 12, 1881, FWC.

48. William to FMB, May 17, 1882, NTC.

49. William to Hawthorne, August 5, 1881, BUC.

50. William to Tupper, May 31, 1882; July 28, 1882, NTC.

51. Taylor to Hawthorne, August 20, 1882, BUC.

52. Anne to Zollie, August 24, 1882, FWC.

Chapter 4

1. Harrison, *Bagbys of Brazil*, 62.

2. William to Tupper, September 12, 1882, NTC; Anne to Mother, September 10, 1882; Anne to Father, September 22, 1882, FWC; Harrison, *Bagbys of Brazil*, 56.

3. William to Mother, September 14, 1882, FWC.

4. William to FMB, December 13, 1882, NTC.

5. William to Tupper, December 6, 1881, NTC.

6. Anne to Parents, December 24, 1881, NTC.

7. William to Hawthorne, January 12, 1882, BUC.

8. William to Dr. Luther, January 23, 1882, FWC.

9. J. J. Ransom to Tupper, January 5, 1880, NTC.

10. William to Dr. Luther, September 19, 1882, FWC.

11. William to Mother, October 13, 1882, FWC.

12. William to Tupper, October 5, 1882, NTC.

13. William to Tupper, October 19, 1882, NTC.

14. William to Sister Ermine, November 20, 1882, FWC.

15. Harrison, *Bagbys of Brazil*, 56.

16. Anne to Father, October 30, 1882, FWC.

17. Crabtree, *Baptists in Brazil*, 44.

18. William L. Pitts, "Baptist Beginnings in Brazil," *Baptist History and Heritage* 17 (1982): 13.

19. William to Sister Ermine, December 31, 1882, FWC.

20. William to Sister Ermine, January 31, 1883, FWC.

21. William to Hawthorne, February 20, 1883, BUC.

22. Harrison, *Bagbys of Brazil*, 58.

23. William to Tupper, December 25, 1882, NTC.

24. Anne to Hawthorne, December 26, 1882, BUC.

25. Anne to Parents, January 3, 1883, FWC.

26. Anne to Mother, March 15, 1883, FWC.

27. Anne to Parents, April 16, 1883, FWC.

28. Anne to Zollie, March 8, 1883, FWC.

29. Anne to Father, April 18, 1883, FWC.

30. Anne to William's Parents, August 22, 1883, FWC.

31. Anne to Father, May 24, 1884, FWC.

32. Taylor, "Rise and Progress," 18.

33. Emilio Willems, *Followers of the New Faith: Culture Change and the Rise of Protestantism in Brazil and Chile* (Nashville: Vanderbilt University Press, 1967), 236.

34. Laird Thomas Hites, "An Investigation of Southern Baptist Mission Work in Rio de Janeiro, Brazil" (Ph.D. diss., University of Chicago, 1925), 129.

35. Loren M. and Alice W. Reno, *Reminiscences: Twenty-Five Years in Victoria, Brazil* (Richmond: Educational Department of Southern Baptist Foreign Mission Board, 1930), 137.

36. Taylor, "Rise and Progress," 24.

37. *Ibid.*, 27.

38. Miguel Rizzo, Jr., "Brazil Welcomes Protestantism," *The Christian Century* 60 (March 31, 1943): 391-92.

39. Harriet Aileen Odom, "The Church at Work in Brazilian Society Through Dr. and Mrs. W. B. Bagby" (M.A. thesis, Baylor University, 1952), 23.

40. William H. Berry, *A Survey of the Baptist Work Within the Territory of the South Brazil Mission* (Rio de Janeiro: South Brazil Mission, 1956), 6.

41. Hites, "An Investigation," 298.

42. Pitts, "Baptist Beginnings," 16.

43. Taylor, "Rise and Progress," 31.

44. *Ibid.*, 155.

45. *Ibid.*, 152.

46. Z. C. Taylor to Willingham, September 3, 1906, NTC.

47. William to Mother, February 18, 1883, FWC.

48. Samuel Gammon, *The Evangelical Invasion of Brazil* (Richmond: Presbyterian Committee of Publication, 1910), 119.

49. Davis, "Missionary Relationships," 72. Hugh Clarence Tucker, a contemporary of Bagby and Taylor, for example, served the American Bible Society from 1887 until 1934 and was directly responsible for the distribution of two and a half million copies of the Scriptures in Brazil. Creighton Lacy, *The Word Carrying Giant: The Growth of the American Bible Society, 1816-1966* (South Pasadena, CA: William Carey Library, 1977), 195.

50. William to Dr. Luther, February 8, 1883, FWC.

51. W. B. Bagby, "Annual Report," March 30, 1884, NTC; William to Sister Ermine, January 31, 1883, FWC; Taylor, "Rise and Progress," 34, 97; William to Dr. Luther, January 12, 1883, FWC.

52. Taylor, "Rise and Progress," 47.

53. W. B. Bagby, "Letter," *Foreign Mission Journal* 14 (July 1883): 168.

54. William to Tupper, September 7, 1883, FWC.

55. W. B. Bagby, "Letter," *Foreign Mission Journal* 15 (October 1883): 170.

56. William to Mother, May 9, 1883, FWC.

57. W. B. Bagby, "Letter," *Foreign Mission Journal* 15 (August 1883): 169.

58. Patricia Summerlin Martin, "Hidden Work: Baptist Women in Texas, 1880-1890" (Ph.D. diss., Rice University, 1982), 84.

59. Robert A. Baker, *The Blossoming Desert: A Concise History of Texas Baptists* (Waco, TX: Word Books, 1970), 135.

60. *Ibid.*

61. Carroll, *History of Texas Baptists,* 599.

62. *Ibid.*

63. James L. Walker, *History of the Waco Baptist Association of Texas* (Waco, TX: Byrne-Hill Printing House, 1897), 95.

64. Tupper, *Decade,* 906. The three other states that increased their giving were Missouri, North Carolina, and Mississippi. Examples of declining gifts included West Virginia ($195,431.11 to $116,964.79) and South Carolina ($100,010.82 to $82,564.71).

65. Hawthorne to Anne, September 17, 1882, FWC.

66. B. F. Riley, *History of the Baptists of Texas: A Concise Narrative of the Baptist Denomination in Texas* (Dallas, TX: By the author, 1907), 64.

67. W. B. Bagby, "Letter," *Foreign Mission Journal* 15 (June 1884): 191.

68. Martin, "Hidden Work," 197.

69. Mrs. W. J. J. Smith, *A Centennial History of the Baptist Women of Texas: 1830-1930* (Houston, TX: Baptist Mission Press, 1933), 177.

70. James W. Bruner, *Progress and Plans of Baptist Schools in Texas* (Dallas, TX: By the author, 1948), 18; Dorothea Gingrich, *Mary Hardin-Baylor College, Belton, Texas and Latin American Relations* (Belton, TX: The College, 1944), 3-15; Mrs. B. A. Copass, "The Women and Their Work," chap. in *Centennial Story of Texas Baptists* ed. L. R. Elliot (Dallas, TX: Executive Board of the Baptist General Convention of Texas, 1936), 236.

71. Charles C. Carroll, "The Origin and Growth of the Foreign Mission Volunteer Band at Baylor University, 1900-1916" (M.A. thesis, Baylor University, 1981), 120.

72. *Ibid.*, 39.

73. *Ibid.*, 108.

74. Crabtree, "Missionary Organizer," 18; William to Anne, October 9, 1886, FWC.

75. Patricia R. Hill, *The World Their Household: The American Woman's Foreign Mission Movement and Cultural Transformation, 1870-1920* (Ann Arbor: University of Michigan, 1985), 85.

76. *Ibid.*

77. William to Tupper, November 13, 1886, FWC.

78. William to Anne, letters from March 27, 1886 through March 29, 1897, FWC.

79. Carroll, *Texas Baptists,* 604-05. The Foreign Mission Board listed the state of birth for missionaries during this period instead of the state where they were located when appointed. As a result, missionaries like Anne Luther Bagby

and Kate Crawford Taylor were not listed as Texans in the Foreign Mission Board tables.

80. William to Texas Baptists, January 17, 1884, FWC.

81. William to Sister Ermine, January 31, 1883, FWC.

82. William to Dr. Luther, February 20, 1883, FWC.

83. W. B. Bagby, "Autobiography," September 1, 1882, FWC.

84. Harrison, *Bagbys of Brazil*, 65.

85. Anne to Father, May 1, 1884, FWC.

86. Zaqueu Moreira de Oliveira, "Persecution of Brazilian Baptists and Its Influence on Their Development" (Ph.D. diss., Southwestern Baptist Theological Seminary, 1971): 29.

87. Horace Victor Davis, "The Missionary Relationships of Southern Baptists with Brazilian Baptists: With Special Emphasis upon the Period Beginning in 1950" (Th.M. thesis, Southeastern Baptist Theological Seminary, 1972), 71.

88. *Ibid.*, 10.

89. Henry H. Keith and S. F. Edwards, eds., *Conflict and Continuity in Brazilian Society* (Columbia: University of South Carolina, 1967), 113.

90. Robert E. Lodwick, *The Significance of the Church-State Relationship to an Evangelical Program in Brazil* (Cuernavaca, Mexico: Centro Intercultural de Documentacíon, 1969), 80.

91. John J. Considine, ed., *The Church in the New Latin America* (Notre Dame, Indiana: Fides Publishers, 1964), 171-72.

92. W. B. Bagby, "Letter," *Foreign Mission Journal* 14 (October 1882): 159.

93. Lodwick, *Church-State Relationship*, 88.

94. Bagby quoted in Albert Benjamin Oliver, *Baptists Building in Brazil* (Nashville: Broadman Press, 1942), 37.

95. *Ibid.*

96. William to Sister Ermine, December 31, 1882, FWC.

97. William to Texas Baptist, February 28, 1884, FWC.

98. *Ibid.*

99. *Ibid.*

100. W. B. Bagby, "Letter," *Foreign Mission Journal* 15 (April 1884): 189.

101. *Ibid.*

102. Willems, *Followers of a New Faith*, 36.

103. Bagby, "Letter," (April 1884): 189.

104. Robert T. Handy, *A Christian America: Protestant Hopes and Historical Realities* (New York: Oxford University Press, 1971), 103.

105. William Warren Sweet, *The Story of Religion in America* (New York: Harper and Brothers, 1950), 345.

106. W. B. Bagby, "Roman Catholicism in America," Sermon, July 1, 1890, FWC.

107. Kate Taylor, "Diary," August 26, 1883, BUC.

108. Anne to Mother, July 1, 1883, FWC.

109. Kate Taylor, "Diary," August 25, 1883, BUC.

110. Kate to Anne, November 22, 1885, BUC.

111. William to Hawthorne, February 20, 1883, BUC.

112. William to Hawthorne, April 17, 1883, BUC.

113. William to Tupper, November 28, 1883, NTC.

114. Anne to Mother, December 28, 1883, FWC.

115. William to Tupper, January 4, 1884, NTC.

116. William to FMB, January 4, 1884, NTC.

117. William to Dr. Luther, January 15, 1884, FWC.

118. W. B. Bagby, "Letter," (June 1884): 191.

119. COSAM, April 7, 1884, RVC.

Chapter 5

1. Irvine to Willingham, June 15, 1897, NTC.

2. Pitts, "Baptist Beginnings," 16; Harrison, *Bagbys of Brazil*, 73.

3. Crabtree, "Missionary Organizer," 12.

4. Z. C. Taylor, "Letter," *Foreign Mission Journal* 16 (October 1884): 195; Mina Everett, "Letter," *Foreign Mission Journal* 18 (November 1886): 220.

5. W. B. Bagby, "Letter," *Foreign Mission Board* 16 (January 1885): 198; *Ibid.*, "The Death of Antonio Teixeira D'Albuquerque," *Foreign Mission Journal* 18 (June 1887): 226.

6. Lester Carl Bell, *Which Way in Brazil* (Nashville: Convention Press, 1965), 35; Crabtree, *Baptist in Brazil*, 6; W. B. Bagby, "Letter," *Foreign Mission Journal* 16 (June 1885): 203; Crabtree, "Missionary Organizer," 6; Harrison, *Bagbys of Brazil*, 73.

7. W. B. Bagby, "Letter," (June 1885): 203; Estep, *Whole World Whole Gospel*, 127.

8. Hites, "An Investigation," 180.

9. William to Sister Ermine, September 11, 1885; William to Anne, April 24, 1886; William to Anne, November 24, 1886; Anne to Parents, July 11, 1887; Anne to Parents, December 27, 1889, FWC.

10. W. B. Bagby, "Letter," (June 1885): 203; William to Tupper, December 7, 1885, NTC; T. B. Ray and others, eds., *Southern Baptist Foreign Missions* (Nashville: Sunday School Board of the Southern Baptist Convention, 1910), 176; Odam, "Church at Work," 117.

11. Crabtree, *Baptists in Brazil*, 54.

12. Harrison, *Bagbys of Brazil*, 75.

13. *Ibid.*

14. Anne to Father, March 27, 1888, FWC.

15. Wright, *Missionary Work*, 218; Harrison, *Bagbys of Brazil*, 75.

16. William to Tupper, February 14, 1886, NTC.

17. *Ibid.*

18. William to Anne, March 27, 1886; April 5, 1886; February 10, 1887, FWC; William to Tupper, February 28, 1887, NTC; COSAM, April 5, 1886, RVC.

19. William to Anne, May 7, 1886, FWC.

20. William to Anne, November 16, 1886, FWC.

21. William to Anne, November 26, 1886, FWC.

22. William to Parents, May 14, 1887, FWC.

23. Anne to Parents, July 11, 1887, FWC.

24. William to Tupper, January 17, 1887, NTC.

25. William to Anne, January 10, 1887, FWC.

26. William to Tupper, April 26, 1887, NTC.

27. William to Sister Ermine December 20, 1887, FWC.

28. William to Sister Ermine, March 24, 1888; Anne to Father, March 27, 1888; William to Sister Ermine, May 21, 1888, FWC.

29. Anne to Parents, December 13, 1888, FWC.

30. Wright, *Missionary Work*, 223; Clayborn Ellis Landers, *Emma Morton Ginsburg: The Wife of the Wandering Jew* (Kansas City: By the author, 1950), 5.

31. William to Sister Ermine, May 21, 1888, FWC.

32. Anne to Tupper, December 25, 1889, NTC.

33. Muirhead, "Evangelical Christianity," 134; COSAM, January 6, 1890, RVC.

34. William to Tupper, December 18, 1889, NTC.

35. Anne to Parents, December 27, 1889, FWC.

36. Anne to Tupper, April 11, 1890, NTC.

37. W. B. Bagby, "Letter," *Foreign Mission Journal* 21 (October 1889): 255.

38. Robin A. Humphreys, *Latin America* (Oxford: The Clarendon Press, 1941), 14.

39. William to Sister Ermine, November 22, 1889, FWC.

40. Crabtree, "Missionary Organizer," 23; *Ibid.*, *Baptists in Brazil*, 60; Harrison, "Memoirs," 144.

41. Jorge Abel Camacho, *Brazil: An Interim Assessment* (London: Royal Institute of International Affairs, 1952), 42.

42. Willems, *Followers*, 165.

43. Taylor, "Rise and Progress," 102.

44. Max Weber, *The Protestant Ethic and the Spirit of Capitalism* (London: George Allen and Unwin, 1930), 35.

45. Clifford E. Ohlmstead, *Religion in America: Past and Present* (Englewood Cliffs: Prentice-Hall, 1961), 134; William H. Brackney, ed., *Baptist Life and Thought: 1600-1980* (Valley Forge: Judson Press, 1983), 255.

46. T. B. Ray, "The Baptist Message in Latin-America" *Home and Foreign Fields* 1 (November 1916): 6-8.

47. Robert Norman Nash, Jr., "The Influence of American Myth on Southern Baptist Foreign Missions: 1845-1945" (Ph.D. diss., Southern Baptist Seminary, 1985): 289.

48. Hites, "An Investigation," 192.

49. Hugh Miller Thompson, *The World and the Man* (New York: Thomas Whittaker, 1890), 36.

50. Charles W. Forman, "Evangelization and Civilization: Protestant Missionary Motivation in the Imperialist Age," *International Bulletin of Missionary Research* 6 (1982): 54.

51. Olmstead, *Religion in America*, 134.

52. Charles Wagley, *An Introduction to Brazil* (New York: Columbia University, 1963), 249.

53. Willems, *Followers of the New Faith*, 248.

54. T. B. Ray, *Only a Missionary* (Richmond: Educational Department, Foreign Mission Board, Southern Baptist Convention, 1927), 16.

55. John R. Sampey, "The People of Brazil: Potentialities, Problems and

Needs of This Great and Growing Nation" *Home and Foreign Fields* 10 (January 1926): 13.

56. Hites, "An Investigation," 139.

57. Flavio Marconi Lemos Monteiro, "Radicalism in Pernambuco: A Study of the Relationship Between Nationals and Southern Baptist Missionaries in the Brazilian Baptist Struggle for Autonomy" (M.A. thesis, Baylor University, 1991), 160.

58. Vining, "Adventures," 2.

59. William Buck Bagby, "W.M.U. Work in South America," FWC; Crabtree, *Baptists in Brazil*, 62, 139; Everett Gill, *Pilgrimage to Brazil* (Nashville: Broadman Press, 1954), 23.

60. *Ibid.*

61. Ruth A. Tucker, *Guardians of the Great Commission: The Story of Women in Modern Missions* (Grand Rapids: Academie Books, 1988), 99; Catherine B. Allen, *A Century to Celebrate: History of Woman's Missionary Union* (Birmingham: Woman's Missionary Union, 1987), 41.

62. Mrs. J. W. Byars, "The Fort Worth Training School," *Home and Foreign Fields* 3 (April 1919): 110-11; Copass, Women and Their Work, 236; Allen, *Century to Celebrate*, 266, 365.

63. Hill, *Household*, 2.

64. *Ibid.*, 60.

65. *Ibid.*, 41.

66. Forman, "Evangelization and Civilization," 55.

67. Tucker, *Guardians*, 63.

68. Hill, *Household*, 63.

69. Robert Leonard McIntyre, "Portrait of Half a Century" (Th.D. diss., Princeton Theological Seminary, 1959), 54.

70. Ermine Bagby, "American Womanhood Before the World," *Home and Foreign Fields* 13 (September 1929): 26.

71. *Ibid.*

72. *Ibid.*

73. *Ibid.*

74. *Ibid.*

75. Anne to Sister, October 14, 1889, FWC; "Report of the Rio Janeiro, Brazil Mission for 1890," January 1, 1891, NTC; William to Anne, June 20, 1895; William to Willingham, March 6, 1897, FWC.

76. William to Anne, January 23, 1891; William to Anne, May 11, 1891; William to Anne, April 22, 1898, FWC; Minutes, Committee on New Missions and Missionaries, July 6, 1891; COSAM, January 22, 1895; COSAM, April 9, 1901; William to Tupper, May 23, 1892; William to Willingham, March 26, 1894; William to Ginsburg, August 31, 1894; Entzminger to FMB, July 10, 1900, NTC.

77. Anne to Sister, October 14, 1889; William to Parents, October 26, 1889, FWC; William to Tupper, November 2, 1889; Soper to Tupper, May 3, 1890; William to Tupper, May 31, 1890; W. B. Bagby, "Report of the Rio Janeiro, Brazil Mission for 1890," January 1, 1891, NTC.

78. Anne to Precious Loved Ones, July 19, 1889; Anne to Dottie, August

10, 1889, FWC; Emma Morton to Tupper, April 17, 1890; William to Tupper, August 8, 1890; William to Tupper, November 2, 1890; Report of the Rio Janeiro, Brazil Mission for 1890, January 1, 1891; Soper to Bell, February 16, 1891; William to Tupper, July 14, 1892, NTC; COSAM, January 19, 1897, RVC.

79. Solomon L. Ginsburg, *A Missionary Adventure: An Autobiography* (Nashville: Baptist Sunday School Board, Southern Baptist Convention, 1921), 94.

80. Crabtree, *Baptists in Brazil*, 94.

81. William to Willingham, May 15, 1899, NTC.

82. *Ibid.*

83. COSAM, May 2, 1899, RVC.

84. William to Willingham, January 24, 1900, NTC.

85. L. M. Bratcher, *Francisco Fulgencio Soren: Christ's Interpreter to Many Lands* (Nashville: Broadman Press, 1938), 21-46; Crabtree, "Missionary Organizer," 20; William to Willingham, May 30, 1899, NTC.

86. Shepard to Ray, April 1, 1909, NTC.

87. William to Shepard, October 30, 1912; Solomon Ginsburg, "A Memorable Month in Brazil," January 17, 1916, NTC; COSAM, October 18, 1913, RVC.

88. Crabtree, *Baptists in Brazil*, 94; Oliver, *Baptist Building*, 63.

89. William to FMB, "Report of Rio de Janeiro Mission, 1890," June 1, 1890, NTC.

90. Z. C. Taylor, "Letter," *Foreign Mission Journal* 26 (May 1895): 10.

91. W. B. Bagby, "Letter," *Foreign Mission Journal* 46 (November 1895): 2; Z. C. Taylor, "Bahia Mission Report," June 1, 1895; William to Willingham, August 2, 1895, NTC.

92. William to Willingham, January 28, 1896, NTC.

93. William to Willingham, June 13, 1896, NTC.

94. William to Willingham, November 19, 1898, NTC.

95. W. W. Barnes, *The Southern Baptist Convention* (Nashville: Broadman Press, 1954), 113.

96. Carroll, *History of Texas Baptists*, 596.

97. Baker, *The Blossoming Desert*, 157.

98. William to Willingham, February 8, 1895, NTC.

99. William to Tupper, April 18, 1890, NTC; Anne to Parents, February 7, 1890; March 28, 1890; May 10, 1890, FWC.

100. Anne to Parents, March 9, 1890; Anne to Father, November 22, 1897, FWC; William to Willingham, April 16, 1900; J. J. Taylor and William to FMB, July 10, 1900, NTC.

101. William to Willingham, May 19, 1896, NTC.

102. Anne to Mother, January 29, 1890; February 16, 1892, FWC.

103. COSAM, June 7, 1892, RVC.

104. William to FMB, September 11, 1894, NTC.

105. COSAM, October 21, 1895, RVC; William to Willingham, March 11, 1898; June 13, 1898, NTC.

106. Crabtree, "Missionary Organizer", 14; William to Willingham, August 29, 1894; August 2, 1895; August 4, 1898; W. B. Bagby, "Mission Report," November 14, 1894, NTC.

107. Crabtree, "Missionary Organizer," 15.

108. William to Tupper, September 8, 1890; October 23, 1891; William to Willingham, April 1, 1895; May 19, 1897, NTC.

Chapter 6

1. Benjamin Harris Hunnicutt, *Brazil: World Frontier* (New York: Von Nostrand, 1949), 313. This rate compared to an illiteracy rate among Negroes in the United States of 70 percent and immigrants arriving in the United States of 25 percent.

2. Robert Martin Farra, "Protestantism in Brazil: A Study of the Activity and Results of the Protestant Missionary Movement" (M.A. thesis, University of Nebraska, 1964), 76.

3. Hunnicutt, *World Frontier*, 316; Willems, *Followers*, 234.

4. Fernando de Azevedo, *Brazilian Culture: An Introduction to the Study of Culture in Brazil*, translated by William Rex Crawford (New York: Macmillan, 1950), 157; Lawrence Francis Hill, ed., *Brazil* (Berkeley: University of California Press, 1957), 143; Willems, *Followers*, 234; Harrison, "Memoirs," 86.

5. Muirhead, "Evangelical Christianity," 118.

6. W. B. Bagby quoted in Muirhead, "Evangelical Christianity," 126.

7. Crabtree, *Baptists in Brazil*, 62.

8. Solomon L. Ginsburg, *A Wandering Jew in Brazil: An Autobiography* (Nashville: Sunday School Board, Southern Baptist Convention, 1921), 255; Harrison, "Memoirs," 86.

9. Hayes, "Religion in Brazil," 214.

10. Willems, *Followers*, 231.

11. Ginsburg, *Wandering Jew*, 253; William to Willingham, December 18, 1897, NTC. This was Z. C. Taylor's second wife.

12. Anne to Father, December 24, 1901, NTC.

13. Anne to Father, December 24, 1901, NTC; Gingrich, *Latin American Relations*, 9.

14. Anne to Willingham, July 15, 1905, NTC.

15. William to Willingham, March 7, 1905, NTC.

16. Anne to Willingham, July 15, 1905, NTC.

17. William to FMB, March 25, 1902; Anne to Willingham, March 25, 1910; Anne to Father, December 25, 1901, NTC.

18. Anne to Willingham, December 25, 1901; William to Willingham, August 28, 1902; William to Willingham, September 6, 1902; Anne to Willingham, September 30, 1902; Sao Paulo Mission to FMB, July 10, 1902, NTC.

19. William to Willingham, April 29, 1903; March 20, 1904, NTC.

20. William to Willingham, November 14, 1904, NTC.

21. William to Willingham, March 7, 1905; Anne to Willingham, July 15, 1905, NTC.

22. Anne to Willingham, November 14, 1906, Anne to FMB, October 1, 1907; William to Willingham, May 2, 1907, NTC.

23. William to FMB, August 12, 1910; April 1, 1910, NTC.

24. William to FMB, November 16, 1907; William to Willingham, July 1, 1908; September 14, 1909; Anne to Willingham, March 25, 1910; William to FMB, April 1, 1910, NTC; COSAM, April 15, 1910, RVC.

25. William to Willingham, December 16, 1909, NTC.

26. Anne to Willingham, August 31, 1910, NTC.

27. William to Willingham, April 16, 1910; May 29, 1910; August 12, 1910, NTC.

28. Harrison, *Bagbys of Brazil*, 131.

29. William to Willingham, December 16, 1909, NTC; Oliver, *Baptists Building*, 88; William to McDaniel, July 14, 1909, NTC; Anne to Willingham, March 17, 1910, NTC; W. B. Bagby, "The Girls' School in Sao Paulo, Brazil," *Home and Foreign Fields* 1 (August 1917): 302.

30. "Bagby Fund Aids Brazilians," *Mary Hardin-Baylor Monthly*, June 1941, 3.

31. Ronald G. Frase, "The Subversion of Missionary Intentions by Cultural Values: The Brazilian Case" *Review of Religious Research* 23 (December 1981): 185.

32. Pitts, "Baptist Beginnings," 16.

33. Anne to Willingham, March 24, 1902, NTC.

34. Anne Bagby, "What the School is Doing on the Foreign Field," n.d., FWC.

35. Anne to Willingham, November 14, 1906, NTC.

36. Mein, "Contributions," 13.

37. Miguel Rizzo, Jr., "Brazil Welcomes Protestantism" *The Christian Century* 60 (March 31, 1943): 391-92.

38. Crabtree, "Missionary Organizer," 14.

39. Fred E. Edwards, *The Role of the Faith Mission: A Brazilian Case Study* (South Pasadena, CA: William Carey Library, 1971), 5.

40. Z. C. Taylor to Willingham, September 3, 1906, NTC.

41. William to Willingham, July 3, 1907, NTC.

42. Taylor, "Rise and Progress," 147.

43. *Ibid.*; Berry, *A Survey of Baptist Work*, 3.

44. Bell, *Which Way in Brazil*, 90; Horace Victor Davis, "The Missionary Relationships of Southern Baptists with Brazilian Baptists: With Special Emphasis upon the Period Beginning in 1950" (Th.M. thesis, Southeastern Baptist Theological Seminary, 1972), 81.

45. Crabtree, *Baptist in Brazil*, 127.

46. W. B. Bagby, quoted in Crabtree, "Missionary Organizer," 17.

47. William to FMB, September 27, 1907, NTC.

48. William to Anne, April 3, 1908; April 9, 1908, FWC.

49. Bell, *Which Way in Brazil*, 96. Basil Miller, *Ten Famous Missionaries* (Grand Rapids: Zondervan, 1949), 20.

50. COSAM, February 14, 1908, RVC.

51. W. B. Bagby, *Brazil: Its People and Their Evangelization* (Richmond: Foreign Mission Board, Southern Baptist Convention, 1900), 5.

52. William to Willingham, September 30, 1902, NTC.

53. Crabtree, "The Missionary Organizer," 15. William published a paper called "The Brazilian Baptist," Z. C. Taylor distributed "The New Life," while Solomon Ginsburg circulated "The Good News."

54. Bagby, "Minutes of the Brazilian Publication Society," November 21, 1905; William to Willingham, December 1, 1905, NTC.

55. Anne to Willingham, March 18, 1898, NTC.

56. Anne to Willingham, March 18, 1898, NTC.

57. COSAM, October 8, 1908, RVC.

58. William to Willingham, July 5, 1910, NTC. Davis, "Missionary Relationships," 81.

59. William to Willingham, November 14, 1904, NTC.

60. William to Willingham, March 20, 1904, NTC.

61. Bertoldo Gatz, "Ministerial Training For Baptist Churches in the State of Sao Paulo, Brazil" (D.Min. project, Fuller Theological Seminary, 1989), 71; William to Willingham, February 15, 1904, NTC. Subjects at the "Bible Institutes" included: Sunday School Work, Doctrines, Baptist History, Evangelism, Homiletics, and Women Missionary Union work. Teachers included: T. C. Bagby, Paul Porter, Pedro Gomes de Melo, Helen Bagby, Solomon Ginsburg, and Emma Morton Ginsburg.

62. William to Willingham, June 1, 1904, NTC.

63. William to FMB, "Seminary Site Proposal," November 1, 1906, NTC.

64. Landers, *Emma Morton Ginsburg*, 13. Shepard had been on the field for only a year when the convention appointed him as college and seminary president.

65. Ginsburg, *Wandering Jew*, 257; COSAM, July 31, 1907, RVC.

66. Bell, *Which Way in Brazil*, 71.

67. J. W. Shepard, "Education and the Brazilian Baptist Missions" *Foreign Mission Journal* 57 (November 1907); 155-58.

68. Hites, "An Investigation," 135.

69. Carr, "Comparison," 66.

70. Ray to William, December 20, 1918, NTC.

71. Frances Marquis Dubose, "A History of Southern Baptist Missions in Latin America" (Th.D. diss., Southwestern Baptist Theological Seminary, 1961), 97.

72. Hites, "An Investigation," 135.

73. Monteiro, "Radicalism in Pernambuco," 145.

74. Tucker, *Guardians*, 139.

75. Harrison, "Memoirs," 93.

76. William to Love, January 8, 1924, NTC.

77. William to FMB, September 17, 1923, NTC.

78. *Ibid.*

79. *Ibid.*

80. L. R. Scarborough, *A Blaze of Evangelism Across the Equator* (Nashville: Broadman Press, 1937), 63.

81. William to Love, December 19, 1923, NTC.

82. Dubose, "History of Southern Baptists," 102.

83. Mesquita to FMB, May 7, 1923, NTC.

84. Monteiro, "Radicalism in Pernambuco," 151.

85. Hites, "An Investigation," 314.

86. *Ibid.*

87. G. S. Dobbins, "The Race Problem's One Solution" *Home and Foreign Fields* 8 (August 1924): 236-37.

88. Monteiro, "Radicalism in Pernambuco," 163.

89. *Ibid.*

90. *Ibid.*

Chapter 7
1. William to Ray, January 1, 1932, NTC.
2. Wagley, *Introduction to Brazil*, 198.
3. Crabtree, *Baptists in Brazil*, 231.
4. Harrison, "Operation Biography," 1; Anne, "Diary," April 29, 1883; William to Sister Ermine, September 11, 1885; William to Sister Ermine, October 17, 1887; William to Sister Ermine, December 20, 1887, FWC.
5. Anne to Father, December 13, 1897; December 19, 1897, FWC; Elli Moore Townsend, *After Seventy-Five Years: A History of Baylor College* (Belton, TX: Student League and Alumni Association, 1921), 44; Anne to Annie Armstrong, May 10, 1899; William to Willingham, April 29, 1903; August 29, 1903, NTC.
6. Harrison, *Bagbys of Brazil*, 123.
7. William to Willingham, April 29, 1903; August 29, 1903; November 30, 1903, NTC; Benjamin Luther Sowell, "Pioneer Parson: Life of Sidney McFarland Sowell, First Southern Baptist Missionary to Argentina," TMs, p. 24, Archives, A. Webb Roberts Library, Southwestern Baptist Theological Seminary, Fort Worth, Texas.
8. Gingrich, *Latin American Relations*, 10; Harrison, *Bagbys of Brazil*, 152.
9. Anne, "Diary," September 3, 1886, FWC.
10. Anne, "Diary," April 29, 1883; William to Anne, August 14, 1886, FWC.
11. Anne to Mother, July 25, 1887, FWC; Harrison, *Bagbys of Brazil*, 77.
12. T. C. Bagby, "Recruits for Brazil" *Home and Foreign Fields* 3 (April 1919), 29; William to Willingham, August 8, 1902, NTC.
13. William to FMB, June 1, 1904, NTC.
14. *Ibid.*; William to Willingham, April 6, 1913, NTC.
15. Willingham to Anne, June 1, 1914, NTC.
16. Anne to Love, November 3, 1916, NTC.
17. William to Willingham, February 4, 1913, NTC; COSAM, June 24, 1913, RVC.
18. Solomon Ginsburg, "Visiting the Sao Paulo Field," Home and Foreign Fields 2 (July 1918): 25; Ray to William, July 23, 1917; William to Ray, November 5, 1917, NTC.
19. T. C. Bagby, "Recruits," 29.
20. William to Sister Ermine, February 8, 1888, FWC; William to Willingham, March 28, 1907, NTC.
21. COSAM, June 19, 1907, RVC; Anne to Willingham, December 30, 1909, NTC; COSAM, February 16, 1910, RVC; Anne to Willingham, March 17, 1910, NTC.
22. Harrison, *Bagbys of Brazil*, 128-30; William to Willingham, September 13, 1912, NTC.
23. Harrison, "Operation Bagby," 1.
24. Anne to Love Ones, August 5, 1891, FWC.
25. Anne to Father, August 29, 1891, FWC.
26. Anne Bagby, "Diary," April 29, 1883, FWC; William to Willingham, September 28, 1911; January 11, 1912, NTC; Oliver to Mother, September 10, 1916, FWC.

27. Anne to Ray, March 17, 1918, NTC; Alice to Anne, December 6, 1918, BUC; Harrison, *Bagbys of Brazil*, 131; Harrison, "Memoirs," 18.

28. William to Ray, December 18, 1919, NTC.

29. Ray to Anne, December 23, 1919, NTC.

30. Anne to Alice, October 12, 1922, BUC; William to Ray, January 8, 1924, NTC; William to Anne, March 28, 1924, FWC.

31. William to Willingham, September 17, 1904, NTC; Harrison, "Operation Biography," 1; William to Alice, October 15, 1913, FWC.

32. William to Harley and Alice, March 18, 1924, FWC.

33. William to Ray, March 15, 1918; Anne to Ray, February 25, 1919; Ray to William and Anne, July 17, 1920, NTC; Harley to Alice, October 27, 1924, FWC.

34. Crabtree, *Baptists in Brazil*, 201.

35. W.M.U. of South Carolina to Anne, May 24, 1920, FWC; Anne to Alice, October 12, 1922, BUC.

36. William to Ray, April 16, 1923, NTC.

37. Ray to William, May 3, 1923; July 6, 1923, NTC.

38. William to Ray, August 18, 1923, NTC.

39. Ray to William, August 21, 1923, NTC.

40. Alice to Parents, July 11, 1928, BUC.

41. Elliot, *Centennial Story*, 235.

42. Anne to Loved Ones, October 1, 1912, BUC; Anne to Ray, February 25, 1919, NTC; COSAM, June 19, 1919, RVC; Anne to Helen, June 25, 1920; Anne Bagby, "Diary," April 1, 1935, FWC.

43. William to Ray, August 11, 1932; Ray to William, November 3, 1932, NTC.

44. Anne to Helen, February 20, 1922, FWC; Alice Bagby Smith, *A Miracle of Modern Missions: A History of the American Baptist College of Porto Alegre, Brazil* (Houston, TX: By the author, 1932), 2; Alice to Mary Preston, January 1, 1932, MHC; Harrison, *Bagbys of Brazil*, 158.

45. Harley to Drs. Ray and Love, December 22, 1924, BUC.

46. Ray to Harley, January 16, 1925, NTC; Smith, *Modern Miracle*, 2.

47. Gingrich, *Latin American Relations*, 11.

48. Gill, *Pilgrimage to Brazil*, 25; Smith, *Modern Miracle*, 4-10.

49. Alice to Mary Preston, n.d., MHC; Smith, *Modern Miracle*, 4; Harley to Dr. Love, September 18, 1926, BUC.

50. Smith, *Modern Miracle*, 7.

51. William to Harley, July 14, 1927, BUC; Alice to Mrs. Rufus Brown, March 11, 1932; William to Harley, August 10, 1930, FWC.

52. Ray to Bagby, February 24, 1933, NTC.

53. William to Maddry, October 26, 1933, NTC.

54. Crabtree, *Baptists in Brazil*, 165.

55. William to FMB, April 29, 1903; October 31, 1903, NTC; COSAM, April 4, 1901; September 4, 1903, RVC; William to Willingham, February 27, 1903, NTC.

56. W. B. Bagby, "Minutes of the Brazilian Publication Society," November

21, 1905, NTC; COSAM, July 31, 1907, RVC; William to Willingham, November 1, 1909, NTC.

57. William to Willingham, July 16, 1908; February 17, 1910; Anne to Willingham, March 17, 1910; William to Willingham, April 1, 1910, NTC.

58. COSAM, March 3, 1910, RVC; Crabtree, Baptists in Brazil, 200; Harley to Ray, July 10, 1925, NTC; Harley to Alice, October 27, 1924, FWC.

59. Ray to Smith, January 16, 1925; Harley to Dunstan, June 4, 1925, BUC.

60. Anne to Alice, September 8, 1926, BUC; COSAM, October 6, 1926, RVC.

61. Alice to Parents, June 23, 1927, BUC.

62. Anne to Alice, December 19, 1927, BUC.

63. Alice to Parents, February 6, 1928, BUC; COSAM February 8, 1928, RVC; Anne to Alice, April 29, 1928, BUC.

64. William to Alice and Harley, July 11, 1927, BUC.

65. William to Alice, September 19, 1927, BUC.

66. Anonymous to Duggar, February 12, 1929, BUC.

67. *Ibid.*

68. Elsi Duggar to Alice, June 25, 1929, BUC.

69. A. L. Dunstan, "Memorandum to Foreign Mission Board," December 30, 1930, BUC. The document was signed by the pastors of four churches in the Porto Alegre mission: Bella Vista Baptist Church; First Baptist, Porto Alegre; the Baptist Church of Gravatahy; and the Russian Baptist Church.

70. William to Executive Committee of South Brazil Mission, January 5, 1931, BUC.

71. William to Ray, January 27, 1931, NTC.

72. Ray to William, February 18, 1931, NTC.

73. William to Anne, June 7, 1930, FWC.

74. William to Anne, July 1, 1931, FWC.

75. William to Ray, April 5, 1932, NTC.

76. Ray to William, May 5, 1932, NTC.

77. Ray to William, January 17, 1931; April 30, 1931, NTC.

78. William to Maddry, December 11, 1936, NTC.

79. Anne, "Glimpses of History: 1880-1940," January 13, 1931, FWC; William to Ray, January 27, 1931, NTC.

80. Harrison, *Bagbys of Brazil*, 144-46.

81. *Ibid.*

82. Crabtree, "Missionary Organizer," 2.

83. *Ibid.*, 3.

84. *Ibid.*

85. Anne to Miss Ford, September 11, NTC; Anne to All, October 11, 1935, FWC; Harrison, *Bagbys of Brazil*, 148.

86. *Ibid.*, 150-55.

Chapter 8

1. W. B. Bagby, "The Use of Opportunities", sermon delivered July 1, 1890, FWC.

2. Berry, *Survey of Baptist Organization*, 133.

Bibliography

SELECTED BIBLIOGRAPHY
PRIMARY SOURCES

Published
Bagby, William Buck. "After Fifty Years." *Baptist Standard*, September 24, 1931, 1.
———. *Brazil and the Brazilians*. Baltimore: Maryland Baptist Mission Room, 1889.
———. *Brazil: Its People and Their Evangelization*. Richmond: Foreign Mission Board, Southern Baptist Convention, 1900.
———. *Foreign Mission Journal, Foreign and Home Fields, The Commission*. Articles and letters, 1879-1939.

Unpublished
Bagby, William Buck and Anne Luther. *Bagby-Luther Family Papers Collection*. Archives, A. Webb Roberts Library, Southwestern Baptist Theological Seminary, Fort Worth, TX.
———. *Correspondence with Foreign Mission Board, 1880-1939*. Southern Baptist Library and Archives, Nashville, TN.
———. *Smith-Luther-Bagby Family Papers*. The Texas Collection, Baylor University, Waco, TX.
———. *Luther Family Papers*. Archives, Townsend Memorial Library, University of Mary Hardin-Baylor, Belton, TX.
Committee on South American Missions. *Minutes, 1880-1939*. Archives, Foreign Mission Board, Southern Baptist Convention, Richmond, VA.

Annuals
Baptist General Convention of Texas. *Annual*. 1885-1939.
Southern Baptist Convention. *Annual*. 1880-1939.

SECONDARY SOURCES

Books
Ahlstrom, Sydney E. *A Religious History of the American People*. New Haven: Yale University Press, 1972.
Allen, Catherine B. *A Century to Celebrate: History of Woman's Missionary Union*. Birmingham, AL: Woman's Missionary Union, 1987.

Andrews, C. C. *Brazil: Its Conditions and Prospects.* New York: D. Appleton and Company, 1887.

Armstrong, J. *Texas Baptist Family Album.* Dallas, TX: Baptist General Convention of Texas, 1985.

Azevedo, Fernando de. *Brazilian Culture: An Introduction to the Study of Culture in Brazil.* Translated by William Rex Crawford. New York: MacMillan, 1950.

Azevedo, Thales de. *Social Change in Brazil.* Gainesville: University of Florida Press, 1963.

Baker, Robert A. *The Blossoming Desert: A Concise History of Texas Baptists.* Waco, TX: Word Books, 1970.

———. *The Southern Baptist Convention and Its People, 1607-1972.* Nashville: Broadman Press, 1974.

———. *Tell the Generations Following: A History of Southwestern Baptist Theological Seminary, 1908-1983.* Nashville: Broadman Press, 1983.

Baklanoff, Eric N. *New Perspectives of Brazil.* Nashville: Vanderbilt University Press, 1966.

Barnes, W. W. *The Southern Baptist Convention, 1845-1953.* Nashville: Broadman Press, 1954.

Bastide, Roger. *The African Religions of Brazil: Toward a Sociology of the Interpretation of Civilizations.* Baltimore: Johns Hopkins University Press, 1978.

Beach, Harlan P. et al. *Protestant Missions in South America.* New York: Student Volunteer Movement for Foreign Missions, 1906.

Bear, James E. *Mission to Brazil.* New York: Board of World Missions, Presbyterian Church United States, 1961.

Beaver, R. Pierce, ed. *American Missions in Bicentennial Perspective.* South Pasadena, CA: William Carey Library, 1977.

Beaver, R. Pierce. *American Protestant Women in World Mission: A History of the First Feminist Movement in North America.* Grand Rapids: William B. Eerdman's Publishing Co., 1980.

Bell, Lester Carl. *Factors Influencing Doctrinal Developments Among the Brazilian Baptists.* Fleming Library: Fort Worth, TX, 1960.

Bell, Lester Carl. *Which Way in Brazil.* Nashville: Convention Press, 1965.

Bello, Jose Maria. *A History of Modern Brazil, 1889-1964.* Translated by James L. Taylor. Stanford, CA: Stanford University Press, 1966.

Berry, William H. *A Survey of Baptist Organization and Church Activities in South Brazil, 1949.* Rio Janeiro: Brazilian Sunday School Board, 1950.

———. *A Survey of the Baptist Work Within the Territory of the South Brazil Mission.* Rio de Janeiro: South Brazil Mission, 1956.

———. *Brasilia Papers.* Rio de Janeiro: Baptist Foundation of Brazil, 1963.

Bosch, David J. *Transforming Mission: Paradigm Shifts in Theology of Mission.* Maryknoll, NY: Orbis Books, 1992.

Bowden, Henry Warner. "An Overview of Cultural Factors in the American Protestant Missionary Movement." Chapter in *American Missions in Bicentennial Perspective.* Ed. R. Pierce Beaver. South Pasadena, CA: William Carey Library, 1977.

Bowie, Fiona, Deborah Kirkwood, and Shirley Ardener, eds., *Women and Missions: Past and Present.* Ann Arbor: Edwards Brothers, 1993.

Brackney, William H., ed. *Baptist Life and Thought: 1600-1980.* Valley Forge: Judson Press, 1983.

Braga, Erasmo. *The Republic of Brazil: A Survey of the Religious Situation.* London: World Dominion Press, 1932.

Bratcher, L. M. *Francisco Fulgencio Soren: Christ's Interpreter to Many Lands.* Nashville: Broadman Press, 1938.

Bruneau, Thomas C. *The Church in Brazil: The Politics of Religion.* Austin, TX: University of Texas Press, 1982.

Bruner, James W. *A Guide Book on Baptist Institutions in Texas.* Dallas, TX: Harben-Spotts, 1941.

———. *Progress and Plans of Baptist Schools in Texas.* Dallas, TX: By the author, 1948.

Burkhalter, Frank Elisha. *A World-Visioned Church: Story of the First Baptist Church, Waco, Texas.* Nashville: Broadman Press, 1946.

Burns, E. Bradford, ed. *A Documentary History of Brazil.* New York: Knopf, 1966.

———. *A History of Brazil.* New York: Columbia University Press, 1970.

Calogeras, Joao Pandia. *A History of Brazil.* Translated by Percy Alvin Martin. New York: Russell & Russell, 1963.

Camacho, Jorge Abel. *Brazil: An Interim Assessment.* London: Royal Institute of International Affairs, 1952.

Carroll, J. M. *A History of Texas Baptists: Comprising a Detailed Account of Their Activities, Their Progress and Their Achievements.* Dallas, TX: Baptist Standard Publishing, 1923.

Cauthen, Baker James. *Advance: A History of Southern Baptist Foreign Missions.* Nashville: Broadman Press, 1970.

Clark, Horace. *An Address Before the Alumnae of Baylor Female College at the Fiftieth Anniversary of the College, June 10, 1895.* Florence, Massachusetts: The Bryant Printing Company, 1896.

Copass, Mrs. B. A. "The Women and Their Work." Chap. in *Centennial Story of Texas Baptists.* ed. L. R. Elliot. Dallas, TX: Executive Board of the Baptist General Convention of Texas, 1936.

Crabtree, Asa Routh. *Baptists in Brazil: A History of Southern Baptists' Greatest Mission Field.* Rio de Janeiro: Baptist Publishing House of Brazil, 1953.

Davis, J. Merle. *How the Church Grows in Brazil.* New York: International Missionary Council, 1943.

Deter, Arthur B. *Forty Years in the Land of Tomorrow.* Nashville: Broadman Press, 1946.

Dodson, W. H. *History of Woman's Missionary Union of Austin Association.* Austin, TX: Capital Printing Co., n.d.

Dwight, Henry Otis. *The Centennial History of the American Bible Society.* New York: MacMillan, 1916.

Edwards, Fred E. *The Role of the Faith Mission: A Brazilian Case Study.* South Pasadena, CA: William Carey Library, 1971.

Elliot, L. R., ed. *Centennial Story of Texas Baptists.* Dallas, TX: Executive Board of the Baptist General Convention of Texas, 1936.

Elliott, L. E. *Brazil: Today and Tomorrow.* New York: The Macmillan Company, 1917.

Encyclopedia of Southern Baptists. Nashville: Broadman Press, 1958. S.v. "Bagby, William Buck," by E. C. Routh.

Estep, William R. *Whole Gospel Whole World.* Nashville: Broadman and Holman, 1994.

Evans, C. E. *The Story of Texas Schools.* Austin, TX: The Steck Company, 1955.

Freyre, Gilberto. *The Masters and the Slaves: A Study in the Development of Brazilian Civilization.* New York: Knopf, 1946.

———. *The Mansions and the Shanties: The Making of Modern Brazil.* Translated by Harriet de Onís. New York: Knopf, 1963.

———. *Order and Progress: Brazil from Monarchy to Republic.* Translated by Rod Horton. New York: Knopf, 1970.

Gammon, Samuel. *The Evangelical Invasion of Brazil.* Richmond: Presbyterian Committee of Publication, 1910.

Gates, C. W. *Industrialization: Brazil's Catalyst for Church Growth.* Pasadena, CA: William Carey Library, 1972.

Gill, Everett. *Pilgrimage to Brazil.* Nashville: Broadman Press, 1954.

Gingrich, Dorothea Lohoff. *Mary Hardin-Baylor College, Belton, Texas and Latin American Relations.* Belton, TX: The College, 1944.

Ginsburg, Solomon L. *A Wandering Jew in Brazil: An Autobiography.* Nashville: Sunday School Board, Southern Baptist Convention, 1921.

———. *A Missionary Adventure: An Autobiography.* Nashville: Baptist Sunday School Board, Southern Baptist Convention, 1921.

Graham, Richard. *A Century of Brazilian History Since 1865: Issues and Problems.* New York: Knopf, 1969.

Harrison, Helen Bagby. "William Buck Bagby." Chap. in *Ten Men From Baylor.* ed. J. M. Price. Kansas City: Central Seminary Press, 1945.

———. *The Bagbys of Brazil.* Nashville: Broadman Press, 1954.

———. *From M.K. to R.M.* Crawford, TX: Crawford Christian Press, 1983.

Hill, Lawrence Francis, ed. *Brazil.* Berkeley: University of California Press, 1947.

Hill, Patricia R. *The World Their Household: The American Woman's Foreign Mission Movement and Cultural Transformation, 1870-1920.* Ann Arbor: University of Michigan, 1985.

Hodges, Melvin L. *The Indigenous Church.* Springfield, MI: Gospel Publishing House, 1971.

Humphreys, Robin A. *Latin America.* Oxford: The Clarendon Press, 1941.

Hunnicutt, Benjamin Harris. *Brazil, World Frontier.* New York: Van Nostrand, 1949.

Hunt, Alma. *History of Woman's Missionary Union.* Nashville: Convention Press, 1964.

James, Preston Everett. *Latin America.* New York: Odyssey Press, 1950.

Johnson, Leslie Leonidas. *It Happened in Brazil.* Oklahoma City: Messenger Press, 1960.

Kaschel, W. *Baptist Ministry and Underdevelopment in Brazil.* Ann Arbor: University Microfilms, 1971.

Keen, Benjamin, ed., *Readings in Latin-American Civilization: 1492 to the Present.* Boston: Houghton Mifflin Company, 1967.

Keith, Henry H. and S. F. Edwards, ed., *Conflict and Continuity in Brazilian Society*. Columbia: University of South Carolina, 1967.

Kelsey, Vera. *Seven Keys to Brazil*. New York: Funk & Wagnalls Company, 1946.

Landers, Clayborn Ellis. *Emma Morton Ginsburg: The Wife of the Wandering Jew*. Kansas City: By the author, 1950.

Lefever, Alan J. *Fighting the Good Fight: The Life and Work of Benajah Harvey Carroll*. Austin, TX: Eakin Press, 1994.

Livermore, Harold Victor. *Portugal and Brazil*. Oxford: The Clarendon Press, 1953.

Lodwick, Robert E. *The Significance of the Church-State Relationship to an Evangelical Program in Brazil*. Cuernavaca, Mexico: Centro Intercultural de Documentacíon, 1969.

Maddry, Charles E. *Christ's Expendables*. Nashville: Broadman Press, 1949.

Mainwaring, Scott. *The Catholic Church and Politics in Brazil, 1916-1985*. Stanford, CA: Stanford University Press, 1986.

Marty, Martin. *Righteous Empire: The Protestant Experience in America*. New York: Dial Press, 1970.

McAfee, Cleland. *The Foreign Missionary Enterprise and Its Sincere Critics*. New York: Fleming H. Revell, 1935.

McBeth, H. Leon. *The Baptist Heritage: Four Centuries of Witness*. Nashville: Broadman Press, 1987.

———. *A Sourcebook for Baptist Heritage*. Nashville: Broadman Press, 1990.

Miller, Basil. *Ten Famous Missionaries*. Grand Rapids: Zondervan Publishing Co., 1949.

Morris, C. H. *The Bible in Brazil*. London: British and Foreign Bible Study, 1954.

Murray, Lois Smith. *Baylor at Independence*. Waco, TX: Baylor University Press, 1972.

Oliveira, Betty Antunes de. *North American Imigration to Brazil: Tombstone Records of the "Campo" Cemetery*. Rio de Janeiro: By the author, 1978.

Oliveira, Zaqueu. *Persecution of Brazilian Baptists and Its Influence on Their Development*. Fort Worth: Southwestern Baptist Theological Seminary, 1971.

———. *Factors Contributing to Baptist Growth in Pernambuco, 1886-1965*. Fort Worth: Southwestern Baptist Theological Seminary, 1968.

Oliver, Albert Benjamin. *Baptists Building in Brazil*. Nashville: Broadman Press, 1942.

Ray, T. B. *Brazilian Sketches*. Louisville, Kentucky: Baptist World Publishing Company, 1912.

———. *Southern Baptists in the Great Adventure*. Nashville: Sunday School Board of the Southern Baptist Convention, 1934.

———. *Only a Missionary*. Richmond: Educational Department-Foreign Mission Board Southern Baptist Convention, 1927.

Ray, T. B. et. al., eds. *Southern Baptist Foreign Missions*. Nashville: Sunday School Board of the Southern Baptist Convention, 1910.

Read, William R. *New Patterns of Church Growth in Brazil*. Grand Rapids: Wm. B. Eerdmans, 1965.

Reno, Loren M. and Alice W. *Reminiscenes: Twenty-Five Years in Victoria, Brazil*.

Richmond: Educational Department-Southern Baptist Foreign Mission Board, 1930.

Renshaw, Jarrett Parke. *A Sociological Analysis of Spiritism in Brazil.* Gainesville, Florida: University of Florida, 1969.

Riley, B. F. *History of the Baptists of Texas: A Concise Narrative of the Baptist Denomination in Texas.* Dallas, TX: By the author, 1907.

Rodrigues, Jose Honorio. *The Brazilians: Their Character and Aspirations.* Translated by Ralph Edward Dimmick. Austin, TX: University of Texas Press, 1967.

Scarborough, L. R. *A Blaze of Evangelism Across the Equator.* Nashville: Broadman Press, 1937.

Shaull, M. Richard. "The New Challenge before the Younger Churches." Chapter in *Christianity and World Revolution* ed. Edwin H. Rian. New York: Harper and Row, 1963.

Smith, Alice Bagby. *A Miracle of Modern Missions: A History of the American Baptist College of Porto Alegre, Brazil.* Houston, TX: By the author, 1932.

Smith, Thomas Lynn. *Brazil: Portrait of Half a Continent.* New York: Dryden Press, 1951.

———. *Brazil: People and Institutions.* Baton Rouge: Louisiana State University Press, 1946.

Smith, Mrs. W. J. J. *A Centennial History of the Baptist Women of Texas: 1830-1930.* Houston, TX: Baptist Mission Press, 1933.

Speer, Robert E. *South American Problems.* New York: Student Volunteer Movement for Foreign Missions, 1919.

Sweet, William Warren. *The Story of Religion in America.* New York: Harper and Brothers, 1950.

Tannenbaum, Frank. *Ten Keys to Latin America.* New York: Vintage Books, 1966.

Taylor, Z. C. *The Land of the Southern Cross.* Baltimore: Maryland Baptist Mission Rooms, 1890.

Titterington, Sophie Bronson. *A Century of Baptist Foreign Missions: An Outline Sketch.* Philadelphia: American Baptist Publication Society, 1891.

Townsend, Elli Moore. *After Seventy-Five Years: A History of Baylor College.* Belton, TX: Student League and Alumni Association, 1921.

Tucker, Ruth A. *Guardians of the Great Commission: The Story of Women in Modern Missions.* Grand Rapids: Academie Books, 1988.

Tupper, H. A. *The Foreign Missions of the Southern Baptist Convention.* Richmond: Foreign Mission Board of the Southern Baptist Convention, 1886.

———. *A Decade of Foreign Missions: 1880-1890.* Richmond: Foreign Mission Board of the Southern Baptist Convention, 1891.

Vedder, Henry C. *A Short History of Baptist Missions.* Philadelphia: The Judson Press, 1927.

Wagley, Charles. *An Introduction to Brazil.* New York: Columbia University Press, 1963.

Walker, James Lafayette. *History of the Waco Baptist Association of Texas.* Waco, TX: Byrne-Hill Printing House, 1897.

Weber, Max. *The Protestant Ethic and the Spirit of Capitalism.* London: George Allen and Unwin, 1930.

Wheeler, William Reginald. *Modern Missions in Chile and Brazil.* Philadelphia: Westminster Press, 1926.
White, M. G. and H. H. Muirhead, ed., *In the Land of the Southern Cross.* Richmond: Foreign Mission Board Educational Department, 1929.
Willems, Emilio. *Followers of the New Faith: Culture Change and the Rise of Protestantism in Brazil and Chile.* Nashville: Vanderbilt University Press, 1967.
Winter, Nevin Otto. *Brazil and Her People of Today: An Account of the Customs, Characteristics, Amusements, History and Advancement of the Brazilians.* Boston: Page, 1910.
Worcester, Donald Emmet. *Brazil: From Colony to World Power.* New York: Scribner, 1973.
Wright, Mary E. *The Missionary Work of the Southern Baptist Convention.* Philadelphia: American Baptist Publication Society, 1902.

Articles

"Bagby Fund Aids Brazilians," *Mary Hardin-Baylor Monthly,* June 1941, 3.
Dobbins, G. S. "The Race Problem's One Solution." *Home and Foreign Fields* 8 (August 1924): 236-37.
Forman, Charles W. "Evangelization and Civilization: Protestant Missionary Motivation in the Imperialistic Era." *International Bulletin of Missionary Research* 6 (1982): 54-57.
Frase, Ronald G. "The Subversion of Missionary Intentions by Cultural Values: The Brazilian Case." *Review of Religious Research* 23 (December 1981): 180-94.
Freedman, Estelle. "Separatism as Strategy: Female Institution Building and American Feminism, 1870-1930." *Feminist Studies* 5 (Fall 1979): 512-29.
Jones, Zollie Luther. "Anne Jaudon Luther." *Baylor College Quarterly,* March 1911, 1.
Harrison, Helen Bagby. "William Buck Bagby." *Baylor Bulletin,* June 1, 1928, 2.
Kang, W. J. "Nevius Methods: A Study and An Appraisal of Indigienous Missions Methods." *Concordia Theological Monthly* 34 (June 1963): 335-42.
Pereira, Jose dos Reis. "And Evaluation of Southern Baptist Mission Work: From Brazil." *Review and Expositor* 62 (Winter 1965): 39-42.
Pitts, William L., Jr. "Baptist Beginnings in Brazil." *The Journal of Texas Baptist History* 17 (1982): 4-16.
Rizzo, Miguel, Jr. "Brazil Welcomes Protestantism." *The Christian Century* 60 (March 31, 1943): 391-92.
Sampey, John R. "The People of Brazil: Potentialities, Problems and Needs of This Great and Growing Nation." *Home and Foreign Fields* 10 (January 1926): 12-13.
Scarborough, L. R. "Marvels of Divine Grace." *Baptist Messenger* (October 22, 1936): 3-8.
Stover, Mrs. T. B. "The Gospel in Brazil—Is it Worthwhile?" *Home and Foreign Missions* 13 (March 1929): 1.
Varg, Paul A. "Motives in Protestant Missions: 1890-1917." *Church History* 23 (1954): 68-82.

Vining, Pet Grant. "Adventures in the Land of Today and Tomorrow." *Baptist Standard* 34 (June 9, 1927): 1.

———. "Fifty Years in Brazil: Dr. and Mrs. W. B. Bagby." *Baylor Monthly* (February 1931): 2-3.

Weaver, Blanche Henry Clark. "Confederate Immigrants and Evangelical Churches in Brazil." *The Journal of Southern History* (November 1952): 446-68.

White, Pauline. "The Two-Fold Mission of the Baptist School." *Home and Foreign Fields* 7 (December 1923): 413.

Unpublished

Carr, H. Joseph. "A Missiological Comparison of the Pentecostals, Baptists and Churches of Christ in Brazil." M.A. thesis, Harding Graduate School of Religion, 1979.

Carroll, Charles C. "The Origin and Early Growth of the Foreign Mission Volunteer Band at Baylor University 1900-1916." M.A. thesis, Baylor University, 1981.

Crabtree, A. R. "The Missionary Organizer." Archives, A. Webb Roberts Library, Southwestern Baptist Theological Seminary, Fort Worth, TX.

Davis, Horace Victor. "The Missionary Relationships of Southern Baptists with Brazilian Baptists: With Special Emphasis upon the Period Beginning in 1950." Th.M. thesis, Southeastern Baptist Theological Seminary, 1972.

Dubose, Frances Marquis. "A History of Southern Baptist Missions in Latin America." Th.D. diss., Southwestern Baptist Theological Seminary, 1961.

Gatz, Bertoldo. "Ministerial Training For Baptist Churches in the State of Sao Paulo, Brazil." D.Min. project, Fuller Theological Seminary, 1989.

Griggs, William Clark. "Frank McMullan's Brazilian Colony." Ph.D. diss., Texas Tech University, 1982.

Harr, Robert Lee. "Development and Implementation of a Relational Evangelism Training Program for Baptist Churches in the Gaucho Culture of South Brazil." D.Min. project, Golden Gate Baptist Theological Seminary, 1992.

Harrison, Helen Bagby. "Dr. And Mrs. W. B. Bagby: A Manuscript Biography." Archives, A. Webb Roberts Library, Southwestern Baptist Theological Seminary, Fort Worth, 1954.

———. "Oral Memoirs of Helen Bagby Harrison." Interview by William Lee Pitts, Jr., Waco, TX: Baylor University Institute for Oral History, 1984.

———. "Operation Baptist Biography Data Form." S.v. William Buck Bagby. Nashville: Historical Archives of the Southern Baptist Convention, n.d.

Hayes, Arnold E. "Religion in Brazil." Ph.D. diss., Southern Baptist Theological Seminary, 1940.

Hites, Laird Thomas. "An Investigation of Southern Baptist Mission Work in Rio de Janeiro, Brazil." Ph.D. diss., University of Chicago, 1925.

Lamkin, Adrian, Jr. "The Gospel Mission Movement Within the Southern Baptist Convention." Ph.D. diss., Southern Baptist Theological Seminary, 1979.

Luther, John Hill. "Removal from Independence of Baylor College, 1887." Townsend Memorial Library, Mary Hardin-Baylor University, Belton, TX.

Martin, Patricia Summerlin. "Hidden Work: Baptist Women in Texas, 1880-1920." Ph.D. diss., Rice University, 1982.

McIntire, Robert Leonard. "Portrait of Half a Century." Th.D. diss., Princeton Theological Seminary, 1959.

Means, Frank K. "Changing Emphases in Southern Baptist Foreign Missions, 1912-1942." Ph.D. diss., Southwestern Baptist Theological Seminary, 1949.

Mein, David. "The Contributions of Baptists to the Life of Brazil." Th.D. diss., Southern Baptist Theological Seminary, 1945.

Monteiro, Flavio Marconi Lemos. "Radicalism in Pernambuco: A Study of the Relationship between Nationals and Southern Baptist Missionaries in the Brazilian Baptist Struggle for Autonomy." M.A. thesis, Baylor University, 1991.

Nash, Robert Norman, Jr. "The Influence of American Myth on Southern Baptist Foreign Missions: 1845-1945." Ph.D. diss., Southern Baptist Seminary, 1985.

Odom, Harriet Aileen. "The Church at Work in Brazilian Society Through Dr. and Mrs. W. B. Bagby." M.A. thesis, Baylor University, 1952.

Scarborough, L. R. "The Relationship Between Baptist Missionaries and Baptist Schools." Foreign Mission Board, 16 June 1936.

———. "The Great Vital Laymen in Brazil." Foreign Mission Board, July 30. 1936.

———. "Rio College and Seminary." Foreign Mission Board, September 1, 1936.

———. "What We Saw and Felt at Sao Paulo, Brazil." Foreign Mission Board, September 17, 1936.

Sowell, Benjamin Luther. "Pioneer Parson: The Life of Sidney McFarland Sowell, First Southern Baptist Missionary to Argentina." Archives, A. Webb Roberts Library, Southwestern Baptist Theological Seminary, Fort Worth, TX, n.d.

Stover, Sherrod Sylvester. "Beginning and Progress of the Religious Educational Agencies of the Baptist State Convention of Minas Gerais, Brazil." D.R.E. diss., Southwestern Baptist Theological Seminary, 1959.

Taylor, William Carey. "Brief History of Brazilian Baptist Doctrine." Rio de Janerio, 1955.

Taylor, Z. C. "The Rise and Progress of Baptist Missions in Brazil: An Autobiography, TMs [photocopy]." The Texas Collection, Baylor University, Waco, TX, 1916.

———. "Z. C. Taylor Papers." The Texas Collection, Baylor University, Waco, TX.

Vieira, David Gueiros. "Protestantism and the Religious Question in Brazil, 1850-1875." Ph.D. diss., The American University, 1972.

Walker, Thomas Thad. "Mary Hardin-Baylor College 1845-1937." M.A. thesis, University of Mary Hardin-Baylor, 1962.

Wood, Mrs. W. A. "Annie Luther Bagby and Her Three Daughters." Archives, A. Webb Roberts Library, Southwestern Baptist Theological Seminary, Fort Worth, TX.

Index